The
JANE EFFECT

The
JANE EFFECT

Celebrating Jane Goodall

Edited by
DALE PETERSON
&
MARC BEKOFF

TRINITY UNIVERSITY PRESS | San Antonio

Published by Trinity University Press
San Antonio, Texas 78212

Copyright © 2015 by Dale Peterson and Marc Bekoff

Thanks to the many people who gave of their time, ideas, and talents
in contributing to this book in its print and electronic forms. Special
thanks to Mary Lewis, vice president of the Jane Goodall Institute
and special assistant to Jane Goodall.

This work has been supported in part by the Radcliffe Institute for
Advanced Study at Harvard University.

Cover design by Rebecca Lown
Book design by BookMatters, Berkeley, California
Cover art: Jane Goodall, courtesy of Thomas D. Mangelsen,
Images of Nature

Trinity University Press strives to produce its books using methods
and materials in an environmentally sensitive manner. We favor
working with manufacturers that practice sustainable management
of all natural resources, produce paper using recycled stock, and
manage forests with the best possible practices for people, biodiversity, and sustainability. The press is a member of the Green Press
Initiative, a nonprofit program dedicated to supporting publishers in
their efforts to reduce their impacts on endangered forests, climate
change, and forest-dependent communities.

The paper used in this publication meets the minimum requirements
of the American National Standard for Information Sciences—
Permanence of Paper for Printed Library Materials, ANSI 39.48–1992.

CIP data on file at the Library of Congress

ISBN 978-1-59534-253-9 paperback
ISBN 978-1-59534-254-6 ebook

19 18 17 16 15 | 5 4 3 2 1

Contents

167 JANE AS EXEMPLAR

Introduction

DALE PETERSON AND MARC BEKOFF

On July 14, 1960, Jane Goodall and her mother, Vanne, pitched their tent in a rough strip of African forest at the edge of Lake Tanganyika in the territory of Tanganyika (soon to become the nation of Tanzania). At the time, only two or three brave or foolhardy men had attempted to conduct a scientific study of wild chimpanzees. These early studies lasted for a few days or weeks, and they were done invariably at a safe distance or from inside a carefully constructed hiding place.

With a casual grace and courage, the young Miss Goodall demonstrated through personal example that those dangerous wild apes could be approached and observed up close and over time by an unarmed, soft-spoken, and lightly dressed human of the female variety. She thus began a revolution in animal studies, one that was soon marked by new discoveries and an unprecedented wealth of new observations. She saw chimpanzees as clever creatures with personalities, emotions, and minds. She discovered that they eat meat and use tools. She demonstrated that their behavior is affected by memory of the past and anticipation of the future. Over time, her work made it clear that chimpanzees are, like us, capable of attachment and loss, willful decision and contemplative self-recognition, honest communication and crafted deceit.

Her celebrity came early, starting in 1963 with the first *National Geographic* magazine article featuring a young Englishwoman living among the apes. That was followed by more articles, then television features and lecture tours, soon reaching large and rapt audiences across the United States. Her 1971 popular book, *In the Shadow of Man*, became an international best seller and was translated into close to fifty languages. Since then, she has been the subject of a seemingly endless series of documentaries, books, articles, reviews, and interviews—sufficient altogether that, with the possible exception of Marie Curie, Jane Goodall may be the best-known woman scientist in history.

Celebrity is not the same as accomplishment, of course, but her accomplishments are clear enough. Her research site at Tanzania's Gombe Stream National Park, on the shore of Lake Tanganyika, is still hosting studies on the behavior of chimpanzees, as well as several other species, and it ranks as the longest-running scientific field station in history. Her scholarly tome summarizing the first twenty-five years of research at Gombe, *The Chimpanzees of Gombe* (1986), remains a primary resource for anyone wishing to understand chimpanzees or to know what happened in primatology during the twentieth century. She has been honored throughout the world for her achievements as a scientist and for her later work in conservation and peace. Add to that a count of references to Jane Goodall in scholarly journals and books, and the testimony of a new generation of distinguished scientists who were her students or were otherwise touched professionally by her influence, and one can soon begin to assemble the portrait of a great pioneer in her field.

Part of the "Jane Effect" celebrated by this book has to do with that professional achievement. Much less known or obvious is the personal side of Jane Goodall. She is an unusually warm and generous person who has always opened her home to visitors, her camp to colleagues and students, her attention to fellow travelers, and her heart to animals and the plight of animals in our contemporary world. The effect of this warmth and generosity is yet unmeasured and untold, and we hope that this book, which was originally conceived as a simple way to mark our mutual friend's eightieth birthday on April 3, 2014, will begin to measure and tell it.

JANE AS FRIEND

In "Who Is Jane Goodall?" Dr. Goodall's friend and colleague Mary Lewis refers to "a thousand facets to the diamond that is Jane." That is an apt metaphor for this woman of energy, creativity, vision, and charisma who shines so brightly, who has done so much in so many ways for so many people and animals, and whose complex personality tends to break down the usual categories.

She is the celebrity who is more than a celebrity, a distinguished scientist open to nonscientific ways of seeing and thinking, the human who has lived among nonhumans. She is a thoughtful adult with depth and sobriety who also possesses a child's psychological immediacy and sense of wonder. She makes herself accessible to people of all ages and sorts, children as fully as adults, and in fact, she often walks about in public clutching a child's stuffed toy monkey. In other words, she is also eccentric—but eccentric with aplomb, so that she usually seems not at all eccentric. She makes decisions about people quickly but is often slow to judge. She doesn't mind strangers calling her by her first name, even though she might easily invoke this or that weighty title. People quickly feel safe and at ease around her, but she is a soldier. She is an activist fiercely dedicated to her cause, or causes, someone who can drop everything for a moment of fun but will not waste a second on trivial matters like rank and decorum. Jane Goodall is, to summarize, unstuffy and nonhierarchical, which lends an extra dimension to her influence on others by way of her impressive talents and accomplishments.

Some may see her as a close friend, while for others she is a colleague, a partner, a teacher, a role model or exemplar, an inspirational figure, or even, when considered at some remove, a visionary: all categories I have chosen to use as a way of lending order and logic to the multifaceted Jane Effect. Yes, the categories are imperfect. They are fuzzy and overlapping. Friends may also be partners, after all, and where does *partner* begin and *friend* end? Is Dr. Goodall a friendly colleague to some or a collegial friend? Yet imperfect categories are not the same as meaningless ones, and I have established several square-holed categories into which, based on my own intuition or general sense of theme, I pound the round pegs of nearly 130 essays.

⋏ ⋏ ⋏

My choices will sometimes seem arbitrary, but for the most part, I believe they are defensible. It seems clear to me, for instance, that Jane does treat a few lucky and interesting individuals as friends first and colleagues or partners second.

I would certainly include in the category of friend Loup Mangelsen, the canine author (with help from Penny Maldonado) of "My New Best Friend." Dogs bring major advantages to the duties of friendship, since they are not the nervously chatty sorts who consider words a substitute for communication. But then, as if to contradict the very idea of alert silence, there is N'Kisi, the language-using parrot who (with assistance and additional commentary from Aimee Morgana) often talks about Jane.

Being a nonhuman creature may give someone a leg up in claiming for a friend this Goodall person. But what can the rest of us do? What circumstances or features will justify someone claiming Jane as a friend? First, I will say that a human friend of Jane's must share a fundamental sense of the seriousness of her mission. She often speaks of the importance of hope, but understanding hope requires one first to understand hopelessness. Given the needs and desires of a human population that has grown from one to seven billion during the last two centuries—and that now seeks energy and resources everywhere from everything—extinctions and environmental destruction will mark our historical moment. This idea is particularized well by Georgeanne Irvine in "Hope Always," who declares that during her thirty-five years of working at the San Diego Zoo, she has seen African elephant numbers drop by two-thirds, black rhinos reduced from 65,000 to 1,000, and the "massive destruction of rain forests and other animal habitats." What or who keeps her from giving up in crippling despair? It is her friend Jane. Irvine tells us, "She is a constant reminder in my life that we can't ever give up."

Hilda Tresz is another serious friend who has done heroic work with captive chimps as the international welfare coordinator of the Phoenix Zoo and through a Jane Goodall Institute program known as ChimpanZoo. She writes movingly about her experiences trying to provide comfort and hope to the chimpanzees who sometimes seem beyond hope. And when she needs hope, she turns to Jane. "She never leaves me hanging," declares Tresz. Erna Toback, who, like Tresz, has worked for many years in the ChimpanZoo program, gives another perspective on being one of the serious friends—and she reminds us that Jane, aside from being "an amazing soul with a terrific generosity of spirit," is also "a regular, down-to-earth human being." Annette Lanjauw adds to the picture, confirming Jane's loyalty and attentiveness to friends in need.

Jane's friendship with Mary G. Smith, once an illustrations editor for *National Geographic* magazine, goes way back to 1962 and a first meeting in Nairobi that Smith recalls vividly and fondly in her contribution. More recent old friends include Fred Matser, Barbara Shear, and David Shear, who all demonstrate that Jane's friends are also "feathers in her wing." That is to say, her friends are almost indistinguishable from her supporters, and they number in the "legions," as Mary Smith writes.

All of Jane's friends are, in one way or another, people she takes seriously in part because they are serious about her and her passions and causes. But no one can be serious all the time, and some other friends remind us of her light side and the wonderful moments of relaxation, peace, and good humor that friendship can bring. Billy Weisman describes, in "Sleeping with Jane," a pleasant night he and she spent on the top deck of a riverboat on the Amazon. Gary "GJ" McAvoy tells how Jane introduced him to the "unrivaled pleasures of Belly Laughter." And Michael Aisner writes of the private Jane he has come to know "after the curtain closes," a person who can be open, thoughtful, conscientious, and sometimes eccentric—as well as playful and fun to be around.

The friends of Jane are there because they, too, love nature and animals, and they accept animals as conscious beings with minds, emotions, and individuality. That perspective is essential, I think, as this section's final two essays—"Animals and Single Malt" by Marc Bekoff and "Jane Magic" by Tom Mangelsen—emphasize. But it still never hurts to enjoy a bit of relaxation, fun, and, possibly, a glass of good scotch in the evening.

—D. P.

My New Best Friend

LOUP MANGELSEN

I live with my best friend Tom, but he used to go away often for his job, so I had lots of other friends to keep me company. Sometimes they stayed at Tom's house with me, and there was one who made me feel especially wonderful. Her name was Jane.

I knew that something very different was going to happen when Tom was getting ready for one of his trips. He was making sure that everything in the house was perfect before he left. People brought in the best healthy food, and everything shone to welcome the important guest. Even the mountains looked as if they had put on their Sunday best in anticipation of the visit. I didn't know that I was to be the host while Tom was gone, but soon a car pulled up outside our little cabin, and the most gentle and elegant lady stepped out. I knew right then that she would become a new best friend.

Jane travels even more than Tom, and my job was to help her relax and write one of her books while she stayed at our home. I decided right away that I liked her and wanted to share all my treasures with her. She liked to play and was great with the tennis ball. I loved it when she threw the ball into the pond so I could go kersplash when I went in after it! I was always careful not to shake my wet coat too close to her when I took the ball back.

We would go for a walk every single day, so that I could show Jane around our neighborhood. She loved everything she saw, and I could tell she was really close to nature. She seemed to understand life from other animals' points of view, and she cared about animals who didn't happen to be human ones—right from her heart. After our walk. we would sit in the sunny office where she could look up at the beautiful Tetons and find the best words for her book about hope and peace. I would lie on the floor as close as I could without tripping her up and watch as she made little notes that she taped to the window to remind her of the good thoughts she was having for her book.

Jane came back to see us many times. Tom would take her to wonderful places like Yellowstone, and sometimes I would go with them in the back seat of Tom's car. We had our picture taken together in all sorts of scenery, but it turned out that the photo of us sitting in the old red truck was the favorite for both of us. It was my job, of course, but looking after Jane for Tom was my best job ever!

LOUP MANGELSEN, World Champion Tennis Ball Hunter and Gatherer, Extreme Pond Jumping Champion, died in 2008 after a brave battle with bone cancer. He brought sunshine and joy to all who knew him. Penny Maldonado helped him write his essay.

Our Friend Jane

AIMEE MORGANA AND N'KISI

Many people have heard Jane tell the story about when she first met the language-using parrot N'Kisi. He peered down at her and asked, "Got a chimp?" I had shown him pictures of Jane in books and told him she was coming to visit. In one picture, she was holding a baby chimp, and N'Kisi looked at it intently. I told him those animals were chimps and that Jane is friends with chimps. After Jane and N'Kisi met, they were friends, too: they formed an immediate connection. Jane called N'Kisi from around the world to say hello and taught him her famous chimpanzee "pant-hoot," which N'Kisi learned to imitate, along with her British accent.

Fewer people know that Jane helped save my life, and one of the reasons she was calling was to encourage me when I was battling a life-threatening case of cancer. Even though Jane is one of the busiest people in the world, she found time to call, listened, encouraged me when I needed it, and helped me make it through that difficult time. She also mobilized others to help, including a South American shaman who happened to be from the Parrot Clan. It meant so much that she took time out of her busy life to be there for me. I know if it weren't for Jane, I might not be here today. Eventually, I came to realize that she was probably missing sleep to talk to me, and I felt guilty about this. But she was a true friend, and I will always be deeply grateful.

Jane has had a profound influence on me, both as a mentor and as an inspiration in my work with N'Kisi. When I was looking for a way to study N'Kisi's contextual communication, I looked to Jane as a model of how to study natural behavior and communication in the context of social relationships. Jane blazed a new trail, showing that it was possible to combine observations with empathy in a rigorous way, challenging scientific dogmas—and she changed how humans view animals. Her work inspires others to follow her example in helping to mend the rift between humanity and the rest of the animal world.

N'Kisi often talks about Jane, and he refers to her as "our friend Jane." He has said many interesting things, such as, "Jane flied in a airplane," adding that "d" to make it past tense, which is a big deal in linguistic terms. Jane has probably logged nearly as much time in the air as a bird, in all of her travels. She has shared N'Kisi's story around the world, including in a television special, and we are very grateful to her. It is a great privilege to learn from her and to see how she handles things with that inimitable grace, and we are blessed to know her. We love Jane and treasure every moment we have with her.

AIMEE MORGANA works with the language-using African Grey Parrot N'Kisi. She is founder and director of the N'Kisi Institute and is on the college faculty of the School of Visual Arts in New York.

Hope Always

GEORGEANNE IRVINE

Animals have always been a part of my life. When I was a child growing up in San Diego, California, I slept snuggled up to a dozen stuffed animals in my bed, explored the canyon behind my home in search of snakes and coyotes, and visited the world-famous San Diego Zoo often. The monkeys, great apes, and big cats mesmerized me, and I loved visiting the reptile house, even though its scaly inhabitants made my mother shudder.

I remember hearing, as I got older, about a brave young Englishwoman who studied chimpanzees in Africa, and then I saw her photo on the cover of *National Geographic* magazine. At the time, I never dreamed I would meet Jane Goodall, let alone become dear friends with her, and I certainly never thought I would have a lifelong career as a spokesperson for wildlife and conservation at the San Diego Zoo.

I first met Jane in the early 1980s when she visited the zoo for a book signing and press conference. I so vividly remember her sitting at a table in front of our bonobo exhibit. Because I was in public relations, I had the privilege of spending private time with her. She must have sensed my passion and concern for wildlife because we have always stayed in touch since that day. Over the years, our paths have crossed many times and our friendship has grown—through mutual friends as well our shared passion for wildlife. Every so often, I received a long, handwritten letter from Jane (and now e-mail), and I have saved every one. A mutual love, respect, and concern for wildlife has bonded us and cemented a decades-long friendship.

In both 1992 and 1993, I spent a month at Jane's chimpanzee sanctuary in Burundi, East Africa, and there I met Amizero, an orphaned chimpanzee who changed my life forever. Jane encouraged me to write a children's book about my beloved chimpanzee. *Hope for Amizero* was written to inspire children and their parents to take action on behalf of Earth's precious wildlife. In fact, Amizero's name means "hope" in the local Kurundi language, so I know it was meant to be—and hope is certainly what we need in the world right now.

During my thirty-five-year career at the San Diego Zoo, I have watched African elephant numbers plummet from 1.5 million to fewer than 500,000; the black rhinos crash from 65,000 to a little over 1,000; the massive destruction of rain forests and other animal habitats; and the bushmeat trade flourish. Although those of us in the conservation field have won small victories, seeing the precious world of wildlife dissolve in front of our eyes is enough to leave anyone—including me—with a feeling of helplessness. What helps keep me going is Jane! Whenever I see her, she speaks of hope for the planet. She is a constant reminder in my life that we can't ever give up. Her voice is etched in my memory—"If we would just give Mother Nature a chance, she will heal herself"—and I believe her.

GEORGEANNE IRVINE is associate director of development communications for the San Diego Zoo. She has written more than twenty children's books about animals.

Have You Seen?

HILDA TRESZ

Have you seen an animal suffer? Have you seen a chimpanzee with a vacant face, sitting in a dark corner pulling his hair out one by one? Have you watched a baby chimpanzee rock back and forth in a corner, hanging onto a blanket so tightly you think her fingers will turn white? Have you seen babies who were just recently smuggled to a different country thrown into an empty cage with other infants, holding onto each other, tandem walking, looking for comfort and safety? These are things I experience daily.

I'm the international animal welfare coordinator of the Phoenix Zoo in Arizona as well as a representative of the Jane Goodall Institute's ChimpanZoo program. My job is to make sure zoo animals are kept in captivity at high standards. Jane lets me know if there is a problem somewhere regarding chimpanzees, and I try to get there as fast as I can to resolve it.

At the beginning, I mostly took care of training and enrichment programs, advised on diet or infant care, helped with basic husbandry. It was not easy, but at least back then I only had to see suffering from a distance. But during the past four to five years I have started to get involved in chimpanzee introductions as well. That is something one cannot do through e-mail, so I have had to experience the horror firsthand. For a social being like a chimpanzee, there is nothing more detrimental than sitting in an empty concrete cage, staring at nothing, hoping someone will say something to you. Hoping someone will even just look at you. Those eyes. I have seen those vacant, sad eyes gazing. Once I got a long hug from a baby chimpanzee who did not even know me. She held me so tight, it seemed for an eternity, craving love in her empty life.

I have seen it all. I have felt it all. Sometimes I feel I'm losing my mind. I feel so helpless, so hopeless, angry, even hateful at times. I have two people in my life who can truly ground me. The first is my husband, who, after I have just seen some horror like that, I call on Skype. I cry while he sits on the other side of the world quietly, patiently waiting for me to calm down. There is nothing else he can do, of course, but it helps. And then, I write to Jane. I don't know how she does it, but she always answers back.

How she finds the time is a mystery to me, but she never leaves me hanging. I wonder how she feels when she reads my e-mail. With all the things she has to do, the last thing she needs is my sadness. And believe me, she gets it all. She has to listen to my pain and frustration, my nagging for help, my constant pleas for solutions, and my turmoil. She is there for me when I'm losing faith in people and losing my mind because I can't help enough and fix it all. And she hits the reply button and comforts me. All the time—no matter what's going on in her personal life, how tired she is, how busy she is, or how sad she is. She calms me down. She looks for solutions. She tells me that I can do it. She pushes me to do more. She grounds me. She is there for me.

She is my friend.

And I turn around like there is nothing wrong, as if I have just seen a new spring day full of flowers, sunshine, and birds trilling.

HILDA TRESZ is the behavioral enrichment and international animal welfare coordinator at the Phoenix Zoo. She is also a representative of the Jane Goodall Institute's ChimpanZoo program.

A Feather in Her Wing

ERNA TOBACK

I fell in love with chimpanzees before I could even tell the difference between a chimpanzee and gorilla. It happened over a two-day period in the early 1970s, while I was ensconced in Jane Goodall's *In the Shadow of Man*, which chronicled her eleven-year journey with the chimpanzees of Gombe. When I finished the last page and gently placed the book on my bed stand, I closed my eyes, imbued with the fantasy of walking the forest paths surrounded by the amazing community of chimpanzee beings Jane had brought to life. By the time I reached Africa some thirty-five years later, old Flo and David Graybeard, the first chimpanzees to touch my heart, had long passed away.

I finally met Jane in the mid-1980s at an event sponsored by the Leakey Foundation, which took place at Cal Tech in Pasadena. Several of us were invited to a reception following Jane's talk. I was immediately captivated by Jane's ease and generosity as she mindfully answered everyone's questions. Although I had a million questions of my own, I spent the entire time carefully listening to her as she responded to all of the questions posed.

When the reception was reaching its end, I gathered enough courage to approach and ask a question regarding the ChimpanZoo program she had mentioned in her talk. Jane's enthusiasm for the program was contagious as she described its mission and told me that a ChimpanZoo program had recently been established at the Los Angeles Zoo. Needless to say, I walked to my car after the event, but my feet never felt the ground.

I immediately contacted the zoo and was invited to meet with the ChimpanZoo's program director, Jennie McNary. I explained that I had recently completed a master's degree in physical anthropology and was deeply interested in focusing my efforts on behalf of chimpanzees. Jennie invited me to return and begin training to observe and collect behavioral data for ChimpanZoo. It was not very long before I was totally engaged and enchanted by the complex social behavior and relationships that played out each day among these captive chimpanzees. In fact, my abiding commitment to enhancing their well-being, whether they were living in zoos, sanctuaries, the entertainment industry, or the private sector, began with ChimpanZoo.

A wonderful tradition began at the ChimpanZoo conferences decades ago and continues today—gatherings between Jane and local FOJs (Friends of Jane) that occur in many cities and towns during her travels around the globe. They are usually held in her hotel room the night before she leaves for her next city and next event.

The ambiance of friends from different times and places is always warm and welcoming. We sit on the floor, on couches, and lounge on Jane's bed, sipping a bit of scotch and water while discussing professional and personal issues and sharing stories about our connection to Jane. Our gatherings always end on a note of hope. Saying goodbye is always infused with sentiment. There are hugs and promises to stay connected. Instead of *goodbye*, I always give Jane a big hug, utter a soft set of chimp *hoots* into her ear—as she does in mine—and say "to be continued."

As a result of these gatherings, I learned early on that Jane is not just an extraordinary heroine or mentor. She is also a regular person. Yes, she is brilliant. Yes, she is an amazing soul with a terrific generosity of spirit. However, Jane is also a regular, down-to-earth human being.

Jane has always said that she could never hope to accomplish what she has alone, without the rest of us in tow. She refers to us as "feathers in her wings." As a feather in Jane's wing, I, too, can fly, aloft and beyond any place I could ever hope to travel alone.

ERNA TOBACK, who worked in the ChimpanZoo project at the Los Angeles Zoo, also taught physical anthropology at Santa Monica College. She serves on the board of trustees at Idyllwild Arts Academy and as a trustee at Chimp Haven.

Charismatic Leader and Gentle Friend

ANNETTE LANJAUW

Jane Goodall is known the world over as a champion for chimpanzees who has highlighted the importance of understanding their intelligence and emotional depth as well as the need for their conservation. Her enormous efforts to educate and engage young people in conservation and environmental awareness have spread around the globe through the Roots & Shoots programs developed by the Jane Goodall Institute.

Many people close to her also know that this work has come at an enormous personal cost. Jane spends countless days traveling from one place to another, giving lectures and telling stories that bring conservation alive and make it relevant to the people who need to hear, who need to feel the urgency in their hearts and minds. The energy this takes, the commitment and dedication, is hard to imagine.

My dearest memories of Jane, however, have to do with the other, less public person. To those she holds close, the less public Jane is a loyal and gentle friend. I was visiting a mutual friend of ours who was going through a serious health crisis. Jane called and checked in every day, just to chat and see how he was doing. She would also check in with me, asking how he was doing and making sure I provided him with the friendship and support he needed. She was on one of her long road trips—and certainly exhausted and frazzled with all the many obligations and responsibilities. Yet her gentle kindness and thoughtfulness toward her friend were so clear. Kindness—and humor, too—are qualities that define her as much as all the professional and leadership qualities she stands for.

Since 1985 ANNETTE LANJOUW has worked with bonobos, chimpanzees, and mountain gorillas in the Democratic Republic of Congo, Rwanda, and Uganda. She is the vice president for Strategic Initiatives and the Great Apes Program at the Arcus Foundation.

My Friend Jane

MARY G. SMITH

On a rainy street corner in Nairobi in 1962, I met Jane Goodall for the first time. She and I, two young women both born in 1934, had no clue then how intertwined our lives would become. Jane had recently begun her chimpanzee project at Gombe under the direction of paleoanthropologist Louis Leakey. Shortly after her astonishing discovery of tool-using by the chimpanzees, she was given a small grant by the National Geographic Society to support her fieldwork. I was a *National Geographic* magazine editor on assignment in East Africa, meeting with the Leakeys to plan a photographic coverage of their monumental work at Olduvai Gorge. Before I left our headquarters in Washington, I'd also been told to size up the young blonde working with chimpanzees in Tanzania. Perhaps, went the thinking, her project might eventually amount to something of popular interest for the magazine.

Jane not only became the world's best-known primatologist, she is also a living symbol for the preservation of our natural world and its animal populations. Her energy and tireless dedication to these very best of causes are legendary. . . . But to turn back for a minute to our first meeting fifty-two years ago: As Jane and I shook hands it was sprinkling rain. She was wearing a blue and white cotton dress with a sash tied in back. She wasn't much interested in talking to me, I recall, and I wasn't particularly fascinated by her either. I sent a letter to a close friend back at the office in Washington saying that Jane seemed nice but sort of frail and that she probably wouldn't last. So much for my ability to read the future!

To this day, when people learn I worked for *National Geographic*, a question I can count on being asked is, "Gosh, did you ever meet Jane Goodall?" Well, gosh, I certainly did. I directed the production of her illustrated articles for the magazine and alerted our television and book divisions to take a hard look at this unique scientist. The result? Three National Geographic books and four television films. Jane and I became close friends. One day she asked me to serve on the board of the Jane Goodall Institute, created in 1977. Later I became its president. Long ago, I asked Jane why she felt the way she did about animals, why she was adamant we should be kind to them. Her answer has always stayed with me: "We should be kind to animals because it makes better humans of us all."

So what's Jane Goodall really like? She's extraordinary, one of the few world-class celebrities who without question fully deserves all the respect and adulation she's received. Jane is a superb scientist and a genuine hero in a world crowded with hero wannabes. But then I suspect her legions of friends and supporters already know this.

MARY G. SMITH, senior assistant editor at *National Geographic*, worked with scientists for more than thirty years to present their accomplishments to a popular audience through Geographic media. She has a special expertise in human and great ape evolution.

My Loving and Inspiring Sister

FRED MATSER

In San Francisco at the first State of the World Forum in 1995, I heard Jane speak. Of course, I had heard about her, but being in her presence was another experience. She used simple language, wore a simple outfit. And she was compassionate, direct, and, above all, warm. After her speech, I approached her, and not too long afterward, I found myself in Bournemouth at the Birches, her family home. In this simple, cozy home, we connected on a deeper level, and I felt included in her family and came to know her very kind mom, Vanne, and her lovely sister, Judy.

Over the years, we met many, many times. Frequently, she stayed at my home, and we sometimes talked until the small hours often about very intimate subjects. She had and has a real and deep interest in people, and she really cares about them. Within a couple of years, she said, "You are my brother." I felt honored to have Jane as my sister and found out about a few more wonderful adopted brothers.

One of our memorable trips brought me to Gombe, where I met many of Jane's chimp friends, including Fifi, Frodo, and Flossi. Jane had also named a chimp after me—Fred. On the very last day of this trip, I went to see Fred, and for one moment we looked one another in the eyes. Jane and I knew that Fred the chimp was ill—and within two weeks after my return from Tanzania, I developed malaria and was on the verge of death.

In the meantime, Fred the chimp died. Jane was sensitive enough not to mention that death, as she was concerned about my situation.

So many supposedly famous people are often stressed and have little time for others. Jane is different. All the times that I have seen her interact with other people, whether it was with the former Soviet leader, Mikhail Gorbachev, or with an unknown African mother, Jane expresses a genuine interest in the person and, showing a deep, inner patience, she always is fully present. She is a beacon of light!

FRED MATSER has for the last thirty-plus years inspired people through co-initiating projects in over fifty countries that aim to give power back to the people in the context of a sustainable environment.

Jane's Personal Shopper

BARBARA SHEAR

When Jane makes her countless public appearances, she always looks elegant and stylish. I'm pleased to say that I once had a role in achieving that look. Although I suspect that clothes and fashion are at the very bottom of her list of things to think about, Jane's typical trousers and blouse look effortlessly elegant on her slender frame, and a colorful scarf wrapped loosely around her shoulders often adds a certain flare. But nothing lasts forever. Jane hates to shop, and Mary Lewis confided in me her concern that Jane's wardrobe was rapidly turning to "shabby chic."

So it was that a friend and I, who had accompanied our husbands to a JGI board meeting in Minneapolis, were given our special assignment. Handing us a credit card, Mary pleaded, "Please go and buy Jane some good clothes and a decent pair of shoes, but don't tell her you're doing it, and for heaven's sake, don't tell her what it costs! She thinks spending anything over twenty-five dollars is extravagant."

We returned with shopping bags filled with good items from a decidedly good store, removed the price tags, and hoped she would think we had discovered a sale at Sears or J. C. Penney. One particularly successful purchase was a pair of very smart white trousers that looked great on Jane. So now, every time I see her in white trousers, I wonder if they could possibly be the ones Maureen and I bought, or if Mary has once again bestowed on another friend the honor of being Jane's personal shopper.

BARBARA SHEAR is an artist and graphic designer who spent many years in Africa. She admires Jane for her extraordinary accomplishments and treasures her as a friend.

Jane and Fifi

DAVID SHEAR

I had known Jane for several years when I took my first trip with her to Gombe National Park, where she began her groundbreaking research. To get there, we traveled on Lake Tanganyika ten kilometers north by boat from the town of Kigoma. As we passed hills denuded by many years of tree-cutting and marginal farming on steep hillsides, Jane talked of her special, almost mystical relationship with Fifi, one of the first chimps with whom she formed a friendship. To use one of Jane's favorite words, it was a "magical" connection, a bond that had lasted for fifty years. Jane told me that Fifi always knew when she was coming to

Gombe. I accepted that this was a special bond, but a psychic one? I was skeptical.

We landed at a small dock near Jane's old house on the lakeshore. She showed me to the room where I was to stay and left, only to return soon after, giving me a subtle sign that I should follow her. I did.

Some four or five hundred yards from the house, up a slight slope and somewhat off a small path sat a chimp looking toward Jane's house and then toward Jane. It was Fifi. Fifi did not move. She fixed Jane with an open face and a benign look. Jane approached the chimp and gracefully moved to sit directly in front of her. Neither touched. They just sat there together in silence, embraced by their special bond.

DAVID SHEAR, chairman of the Jane Goodall Institute of the United States from 2002 to 2008, is engaged with JGI in a long-term program supported by the World Bank and the German Aid Organization to preserve the Greater Serengeti National Park Ecosystem.

Sleeping with Jane

BILLY WEISMAN

While attending a business conference in Brazil about twenty years ago, I had an adventurous encounter with a stranger that permanently altered and enhanced my life. I will confess that I was, at the time, one of six people on the planet unaware of Jane Goodall's extensive body of work or her fame. But I will never forget the moment we met and will always cherish the twenty-four hours we spent together.

This happened in the middle of the world's greatest rain forest, and

I was traveling with a large group of fellow conference attendees who wanted to explore the place where the Rio Negro joins the mighty Amazon. We had each been randomly assigned to one of several small boats for our twenty-four-hour expedition.

As I was boarding the unstable vessel, my name tag dropped into the river. Immediately after that, I was greeted on deck by a cheerfully engaging woman asking, "What's your name?" followed by, "Mary, do you have a marker?" I still have the white safari shirt that has "Billy" handwritten on it, as it marks the moment we met and the beginning of a most exciting journey.

That evening when everyone was exhausted and retiring to their cabins, I noticed Jane inconspicuously climbing the ladder to the top deck. Curious, I followed, and when she explained that she preferred not to sleep in a "refrigerated" cabin, I grabbed some seat cushions from the galley and returned to join her on the top deck. Despite the heat and bugs, the night sights and sounds on the rain forest river were indeed magical, but magical second only to our getting-to-know-each-other conversation. It seems as if, upon hearing our occasional laughter, several others caught on, and soon the deck was full of joy seekers. Then it started to drizzle, and the crowd thinned out. Then the rain came, and it was again just me and Jane until sunrise. When we rejoined the group at breakfast, one of our fellow travelers, David Miller, blurted out, "Billy slept with Jane!"

At the end of the trip Jane signed my safari shirt "Love, Jane"—and so the rumors linger. It's a great story about the night I fell in love with Jane and the principles she stands for. That night I learned about living a life of purpose, and that one must listen to one's own voice . . . sometimes away from the crowd. As the crowds come and go, so will the minor irritants of heat, bugs, or rain. That night I learned to think big and act small, and when alone in the dark, not mind the alligators below and always be guided by the stars above.

BILLY WEISMAN, the visionary, values-based leader of Weisman Enterprises, founded many businesses that have provided outsourced, non–core management services to Fortune 500 companies.

Belly Laughter

GARY "GJ" McAVOY

A few years ago, Jane introduced me to the odd and as-yet-unrivaled pleasures of belly laughter, and I have since found it to be the perfect icebreaker for small groups of people who might otherwise be socially restrained. Try it at your next business workshop. It's a guaranteed way to loosen up the more sober participants.

Our good friend and Jane's spiritual guide, Chitcus, happened to be in town. They know each other well, and Jane must have sensed the sturdy Marine was carrying some burden that needed exorcising, for with no explanation at all she made us both lie down on the floor—arranging us just so—then lay down herself with her head resting on my stomach, while raising Chitcus's head so she could properly scooch beneath it.

Then she just started lightly chuckling, but Chitcus and I were already giggling at the absurdity of the arrangement, so it didn't take much to get us all going. Within seconds, the bouncing of heads on heaving bellies did its job, provoking endless fits of laughter until we were forced to roll away from each other in agony, gulping for air and wiping the tears from our eyes. We were shy one person to achieve the regulation quadrangle, so the chain wasn't complete. But it sufficed.

All of which demonstrates that no matter how old a dame she becomes, Jane retains a childlike joy and will always find a way to bring out the most fun in people.

GARY MCAVOY is a Seattle-based technologist and writer who led the Jane Goodall Institute's Seattle Base Camp from 1999 to 2004. He also worked with Jane on her book *Harvest for Hope*.

How Can Jane Keep Going at This Pace?

MICHAEL AISNER

It's a logical question, of course. She's eighty and doing almost daily what wearies the most resilient souls—the hassles of *travel*. She's been to the sun and back in airline miles with no complaints. Pinch her (lightly). Is she real?

I think I know where she gets her boundless stamina. I proffer that there is an additional and potent ingredient adding to the typical life forces of oxygen and blood—standing ovations! It's not the fact that they are standing. It's the fact that people care. They care to be there, and they care enough about Jane's messages, not just the verbal ones but that she represents something deeply meaningful, so they bathe her in life-affirming bravos. I'm not a doctor, but I think this contributes to keeping her blood pulsing. I contend that she gets more *genuine* standing ovations than anyone else on earth. And I'm not referring to presidential standing "O"s obliged by an office; these are expressions by people who are moved to their feet by what many would admit are mostly intangible feelings. They ovate no matter the venue—restaurants, escalators, airplanes, hotel lobbies, stadia. It juices her soul: all these hands on her back levitating her through her days.

Who is this Jane Goodall anyway?

One thing we know for sure: she's one driven dame. She was driven to go to what then was considered a "dark" continent as a mere lass, even alone if need be, to sit in a forest surrounded by poisonous snakes and who knows what else to try connecting with another ape species. Driven to stay, to get funded, to anthropomorphize her subjects against the wagging fingers of stuffy alpha males. Bold. Driven.

But to really know *who* someone is, especially one with a public persona, you must see her after the curtain closes. When the guard is down, you can peer underneath the facade, beyond the propped-up celebrity. For Jane, those little insights reveal the core of her person. So, here are a few little narratives that add to the story of who she really is.

I saw her spend more than fifteen private minutes with a man she thought was a janitor at NBC. The man was actually Jay Leno in bib overalls before getting his makeup, but it didn't matter to her. She does not value a late-night talk-show host over a custodian.

She once scolded me for asking a man for directions out a car window without greeting him first.

She refused to be escorted to the front of the line when we were discovered by management waiting with everyone else for a ride at Universal Studios.

She felt terrible that because she was the Grand Marshall of the Rose Parade in Pasadena, her police escort caused some disruption.

From her room above, she lowered a basket of fruit outside by bedsheet to her son and me in a fancy NYC hotel.

She disliked the setup when she was talking to *Fresh Air*'s Terry Gross on NPR because they were not in the same room and had no eye contact.

At a Princeton president's reception, she ate flowers off the appetizer tray to the abject horror of the tuxedoed student waiter.

She stays in revolving doors going round and round while you are waiting in the street to leave.

She greets dogs and horses before their owners.

She stays up as late at the youngsters, eyes closed, seemingly sleeping but absorbing everything she hears.

She sat quietly at sunrise waiting for the migrating cranes to wake up and fly.

She giggled and ran around like a little girl when a mother bear and two cubs passed by our window.

She scolded Michael Jackson for wanting a second chimp and Kirstie Alley for keeping lemurs in her home.

She strained her coffee through a nylon stocking.

She was admonished by her mother for not paying attention to her own needs.

She connived getting a dog into the UN by inviting a blind friend and holding the hound high from the sacred UN pulpit, proclaiming, "If every representative in here had a dog of their country lying beside them in all their proceedings, from Afghans to Irish Setters to English bulldogs, this would be a more conciliatory world."

She let her iconic ponytail loose and donned dark shades to dance incognito at a fundraiser.

She knows in a minute if she likes someone. There are basics. A famed LA talk show host who didn't look up when she entered but had her sit down and just turned on the mic for an on-air greeting was not her style. Nor was the ultra-famous CEO at his home who was disconnected and distracted.

She wore a towel as a turban in a belly dancing restaurant while sitting on floor pillows eating.

She marvels at so much of life, inside and out, bearing an almost angelic inner and outer peace.

She snarled on air at Donahue about his phrasing and made Jay Leno laugh at the snappiest quip.

She sends handwritten letters of thanks and little gifts to friends.

These are merely a few footnotes that define bits of her real character and person. She's real, with flaws and weaknesses. A life making a profoundly important contribution to the rest of us—not just in what she does and says, but in what she represents to a world so thirsting for someone they can trust, believe in, and utter the word *hero* to describe. Real heroes seem like vapors these days. So I raise a glass of whiskey (though I won't drink) in her honor, and to Vanne and Mortimer and Judy and Louis.

Oh, I guess I should close with an obligatory Gandhi quote or something, but instead, here's one that reflects on one Valerie Jane Goodall. It's about what you ask of yourself. And for this I go to one of the greatest scholars of all time, who said, "When your heart is in your dream, no request is too extreme." Thanks, Jiminy Cricket.

Since the 1980s MICHAEL AISNER and Jane have not stopped cavorting. After twenty-eight years of getting a "not interested" from Jane, Aisner is now producing a feature film about her formative and triumphant first years in the forest.

Animals and Single Malt

MARC BEKOFF

Back when I was a graduate student at Washington University in St. Louis, I'd heard about Jane Goodall going off to live with the chimpanzees. I also knew of her husband at the time, the photographer Hugo Van Lawick. I'd read Jane's groundbreaking monograph on the behavior of free-living chimpanzees in the Gombe Stream Reserve, and it was clear to me that she was going to make a difference in how animals are studied and the ways in which people refer to them. I pocketed those perspectives, and they have always been in my head and heart over the past four-plus decades.

In the fall of 1971, when I was still in graduate school, an unexpected visitor showed up at my home in St. Louis. It was Hugo. He stayed there for a few days, sharing his bed with Moses, a huge white malamute. Hugo and I had long chats about animal behavior, the importance of observing identified individuals over long periods of time, and what Jane was accomplishing despite a large number of skeptics. Jane's seminal observations of David Greybeard using a tool were met with skepticism until she showed a video of this amazing behavior.

That was an exciting discovery, but Jane's methods and approaches were what I really found so astonishing—starting with her habit of naming the chimpanzees she studied and stressing their individual personalities. She felt that every individual counts, not only among the animals she studied but also when working with people who were concerned about saving other species and their homes. At the time, naming and recognizing individuality were not standard operating procedure in studies of animal behavior, most of which were conducted in various sorts of artificial, captive settings. "Naming animals is subjective and will influence how data are explained," I was told, and individual differences were "noise in the system," while talking about animal personalities was fraught with error. Most researchers engaged in normative thinking about other animals and liked to talk about "the dog," "the coyote," "the chimpanzee," or "the elephant." Subsequent research has shown how wrong they were.

I was vulnerable, of course, as a graduate student, but I had Jane's example to consider. Jane had refused to change the ways in which she referred to the chimpanzees, and I too refused to change. In the end, it worked. And, over the past forty-some years, Jane has proven to be on the mark. Science has changed, and we are now allowed to consider animals as subjects, not objects, and to recognize that their individual personalities are extremely important to study.

I met Jane on a few occasions during the 1970s and 1980s, and in 1999 we got together when she was in Boulder, staying at the home of our mutual friend Michael Aisner. We hit it off, wrote some essays together, and worked together on a book that was published in 2002 called *The Ten Trusts: What We Must Do to Care for the Animals We Love*, which has since been published in a number of foreign languages. Working with Jane on that book and on other pieces was a true joy, and despite her horrific travel schedule, she was always available for talking and faxing. Jane has this uncanny ability to give her full attention to someone despite being pulled here and there. Jane and I also cofounded Ethologists for the Ethical Treatment of Animals: Citizens for Responsible Animal Behavior Studies in July 2000.

When we began working together, she wasn't using e-mail. What a pain that was. But we crossed paths through faxing or phoning, and when I awoke and began working at around four in the morning, she was eating her small lunch or having tea with her sister, Judy, and other friends. I also began to work closely with Jane's Roots & Shoots program as a roving ambassador because I, too, travel all over the world—not as much as Jane, of course. How she does what she does blows my mind, and she is still going strong as she turns eighty years old. I share fully Jane's belief that every individual counts and that everyone can make a positive difference in the lives of other animals and in saving their homes.

Jane is clearly one of the most influential scientists and spokespersons for animals in history. Her original monograph is a classic, as is her later one—the encyclopedic *The Chimpanzees of Gombe* (1986), which summarizes much (by no means all) of what she learned about chimpanzees in her first twenty to twenty-five years of research. But Jane also works closely with human animals, because she understands there's no way to work for nonhumans without figuring out how humans can coexist with them.

On the personal side, Jane and I share a passion for good single malt scotch, and when I meet her, I always bring a small flask of what she calls "cough medicine."

Dr. Jane has influenced my life in many, many ways, and I am thrilled to count her as a close friend.

Thank you, Jane, for what you have done—and are continuing to do—for all animals, nonhuman and human, and for their homes. I carry you and your messages in my heart and will continue to do so forever.

MARC BEKOFF is a professor emeritus of ecology and evolutionary biology at the University of Colorado at Boulder. He has published twenty-six books and more than a thousand popular and scientific essays. He blogs regularly for *Psychology Today*.

Jane Magic

THOMAS D. MANGELSEN

In March 2003, I picked Jane up at the airport in Kearney, Nebraska, which is about twenty-five miles from my family's cabin on the south banks of the Platte River. I had gone there a week earlier to prepare the cabin for her arrival. She had never been there before, and I didn't want her to be too shocked. My mother had long ago abandoned the place, it being mostly a duck-hunting shack used by untidy men. In fact, it had started off as a one-room schoolhouse when I was a kid. Over the years, my dad built a garage, not for vehicles but for duck and goose decoys, boats, and hunting stuff; and onto the garage he put an extra bedroom. Then a few years later, he added an upstairs living room with a stone fireplace, a kitchen, a bathroom, a shower, and a picture window overlooking the river.

Before Jane's arrival, I took down a few of the cobwebby and more macabre-looking duck and goose mounts that my dad or I had mounted. Some were tacked against the walls, others swinging from a single wire from the ceiling. Knowing from our conversations that Jane wasn't big on hunting and dead things, I decided not to freak her out. I moved some of the scarier mounts to the basement, so she would be able to sleep at night—but I soon realized that, short of burning down the cabin, it would be impossible to hide its history as the family's hunting cabin. In the end, I realized that Jane was not that judgmental. She had pretty much seen it all, I thought, so I let it be. I was right. Jane was never critical of how I grew up or of my father, although once or twice she would joke about the follies of my youth. She was right about that!

When she walked into the cabin, the fire was going, and I had a kettle of homemade soup on the stove. She looked right past the dead mounts and out the picture window to the river where the cranes were coming to roost. We stayed up late, working on a bottle of single malt and talking about the cabin, my dad, waterfowl, and cranes. Before she went to bed, she cranked open the windows so that she could hear the birds' conversations through the night. Most mornings she would rise early, before me, and bring me a cup of coffee downstairs where I slept, and we would walk the river road with O'Ryan, my brother's yellow lab, down to the old Uridil farm where great clouds of gray birds rose from their nighttime roost headed toward the cornfields.

After the early morning "fly out," we would go back to the cabin to warm up with another cup of coffee, a piece of toast and cheese, and maybe a fried egg. I learned that eating was not high on Jane's list—and no wonder she is always so fit. I also learned that I could actually live on less food, including meat. Late mornings we would go look for snow geese coming to the marshes in the rainwater basin or to one of the Interstate 80 lakes. Hundreds of thousands of white geese were spiraling and whiffling like falling leaves, dumping the air from their wings in a rush to get a drink. Jane loved their acrobatics and was especially fond of the white-fronted geese, who are the best at whiffling and enjoy it most.

Jane fell in love with the cranes and the river, and she couldn't wait to share the cabin and the experience with those she loved. In March or April, for more than a dozen years, Jane has migrated to the cabin and cranes and has brought many dear friends and family with her to see the ancient gathering of birds and symbols of peace.

I have been eternally blessed a million times more for the many other adventures we've had before and since: prairie dogs and ferrets in the Badlands, snowed in at Spearfish Lodge with like-minded folks, Roots &

Shoots battalions of smiling and joyful kids, parties and fundraisers with Jane's dear friend Pierce Brosnan, and lunch at Marlon Brando's house. One of Marlon's last interviews before he died was of Jane. He said there were three people he greatly admired and wanted to interview: Elizabeth Taylor, Michael Jackson, and Jane Goodall. We were there most of the afternoon, and after the interview I will never forget Marlon wanting Jane to stay longer, but she had to catch a flight. He stood on his front porch, arms stretched wide, hands grasping the open sliding glass doors, saying goodbye to Jane. I turned back for one last glance and saw the tears in his eyes.

That's the Jane Magic. She touches all, no matter who or where.

THOMAS D. MANGELSEN, founder of the Images of Nature galleries, is a critically acclaimed nature photographer. His limited edition prints have been exhibited in the Smithsonian Museum of Natural History, the Joslyn Art Museum, the National Museum of Wildlife Art, and other major museums.

JANE AS COLLEAGUE

When I think of *colleagues*, I imagine fellow workers in the field, educated grown-ups laboring shoulder to shoulder in the same institution or industry and regarding each other generously in the manner of friendly peers. That defining image of *colleague* will have to be modified slightly for the purposes of this section, given that Jane Goodall actually has few peers. Thinking of her historically as a pioneering primatologist, for instance, who were her peers? The American zoologist George Schaller studying mountain gorillas in 1959 comes to mind, as do a few others. But of course, Schaller stayed with the gorillas for about a year before moving on to other charismatic megafauna, while Jane continued with the chimps for twenty-five years before handing the management of Gombe research over to others, who continue the work even now, after more than a half-century.

In this section, the story of Jane's effect as a colleague starts with the essay by Colin Groves, who harks back to Jane's early days as a struggling young scientist. Not yet thirty years old in 1963 and already the world's top expert on wild chimpanzees, she was still struggling to get her union card, the PhD that would mark her as a real scientist. Groves's first impression of Jane was based on the reverberating memory, in John Napier's primate anatomy laboratory in London, of an eccentric young woman who would show up for private tutorials on primates early in 1960 with a pet mongoose in tow. Groves went on to earn his PhD, Jane earned hers, and they remained aware of each other from afar. He followed her astonishing career and was affected both by her discoveries and by her underlying approach, which, he saw, was based on an intuitive understanding of the human connection with the nonhuman.

David Anthony Collins came to Gombe during the early 1970s, representative of a younger generation and another of Jane's many students from that time. He was always a special student, however, both because he studied baboons instead of chimps and because he was an exceptionally astute and engaged human being. Although he paused to complete his education, Collins never entirely left Gombe; for several years, he has been director of baboon research there. Michael A. Huffman, the third scientific colleague contributing an essay, is an American who studied primatology under Junichiro Itani at Kyoto University. Huffman tells of meeting Jane in Kigoma in 1985 and discovering that she and Itani shared "an ability to interact with everyone [they] meet as equals." Craig Stanford writes as another younger scientific colleague of Jane's. He came to Gombe during the 1990s as a postdoctoral researcher and found that what began as a "coveted research opportunity" turned into a collegial association that continues to the present time.

The Jane Goodall Institute has created another network of professional colleagues. The Institute was started in the mid-1970s by some of Jane's loyal friends in California, and its original function was to help stabilize the finances underwriting research at Gombe during a particularly difficult period in Jane's life. The Institute grew, though, and it changed in scope and mission as Jane herself changed directions and, finally, professions—from scientist to activist.

The Institute currently maintains offices in about thirty countries around the world. Jane's hundreds of friends, associates, allies, and colleagues who work at or with the Institute in its global presence are represented in this section by contributors writing from Africa, Asia, Australia, Europe, and North and South America: Paula Gonzalez Ciccia, Polly Cevallos, Peter L. Biro, Federico Bogdanowicz, Ferran Guallar, Peter Apell, Donald R. Kendall, Dilys MacKinnon, Claire Quarendon, Gudran Schindler-Rainbauer, and Phee Boon Kang.

Finally, two more colleagues, laborers in the field and members of the JGI family, George Strunden and Mary Lewis, deserve special mention. Strunden founded and for many years managed TACARE, the project that brought tree-planting opportunities along with other community services to the villages in western Tanzania located around Gombe Stream National Park. In doing so, he provided an important model for how conservation can work under sometimes difficult circumstances in Africa. Mary Lewis is known to many as Jane's right-hand woman. She is a colleague, certainly, and widely appreciated for her talent with people and organizations, but she has also long served as friend, scheduler, and aide-de-camp to Jane as she travels, spreading the message and doing what she can do to make the world a better place. Lewis probably knows Jane as well as anyone, in other words, and her essay provides an inside look at the woman and the community of colleagues that has crystallized around her.

—D. P.

Primate Taxonomy and Chimpanzee Minds

COLIN GROVES

The year was 1963. Fresh from getting my bachelor of science degree, I arrived to do a PhD with John Napier in his Unit of Primatology and Human Evolution at London's Royal Free Hospital School of Medicine. I was fortunate to be studying there alongside a number of people who have become primatological luminaries, but aside from a brief moment when I entered a room where she and John were editing a film to tell her she was wanted on the telephone, I just missed the most luminous luminary of them all: Jane Goodall. Jane had emerged from Gombe Stream Chimpanzee Reserve, as it then was called, to place her early observations in a primatological context, and she and her pet mongoose had spent a while in John's buzzing and exciting Unit. But alas, all that remained of Jane by the time I settled in there were bemused cries of "Mind the mongoose!" and stories of an enterprising woman whose persistence and keen observations had already begun to wake up the rather sleepy field of primate behavior.

Jane disappeared back into the forest, venturing forth occasionally to bring news of her ever more striking discoveries. I remember the sound of jaws dropping, including my own, almost throughout the world when she first documented that chimpanzees were making and using tools.

Meanwhile, as a budding primate taxonomist, I was transported from time to time to various laboratories in the United States and Britain to identify various monkeys held there, mostly in tiny cages, awaiting what fates I dared not inquire. Some of these laboratories even held chimpanzees, in cages only slightly larger than those for the larger monkeys. I felt a twinge of pity for those imprisoned primates but at the time more or less accepted that somehow it was necessary. Jane's continuing discoveries made me rethink my position. Her relentless anthropomorphizing of her wild chimpanzees and her giving them names, although often criticized, had its effect. These apes were undeniably behaving in ways that reminded us of human actions. Surely, if those behaviors among humans were the products of thinking and emotions and reasoned strategies, why should the same behaviors in Jane's chimpanzees not also be the product of similar mental processes? That made sense, but then why were chimpanzees imprisoned in laboratories? And what of the monkeys? How chimpanzee-like would they turn out to be?

And so I was in no position to resist Shirley McGreal's request in 1974 that I join the International Primate Protection League (IPPL), and I was delighted to find my name next to Jane's in the organization's list of advisors. After migrating to Australia, I did my bit—not very much, really—for primate welfare over the next few decades, and I saw the situation gradually improve, especially when Lynette Shanley became the Australian representative for IPPL. I got used to the questions about why a taxonomist should take an interest in primate welfare. After all, a taxonomist looks at the skins and skulls of dead creatures in museums. It was not until the 1990s, when Jane paid her first visit to Australia, that I at long last got to meet her properly. I was happy to become one of those who took Jane from place to place to lecture and sign books, and once, in my home, I even treated her briefly to a cup of watery, unfiltered coffee. Overlooking the tragedy of the failed coffee, Jane dutifully signed my collection of all her books.

Jane's effect on my thinking has been tremendous, but it is just a microcosm of the effect she has had on how the world in general thinks of chimpanzees, of primates, of the whole natural world and our relationship to it.

Taxonomist COLIN GROVES has done fieldwork in Kenya, Tanzania, Rwanda, the Democratic Republic of the Congo, Iran, Sri Lanka, and Indonesia. He has lectured at the Australian National University since 1974.

Jane's Influence on Me and My Life

DAVID ANTHONY COLLINS

I can thank Jane for the whole course of my professional life. Since the day she accepted me to work at the Gombe Stream Research Centre, very little of that life isn't in one way or another attributable to her. Most immediately, she provided the chance to live with nature in the big prism of mountain, water, and sky that is Gombe. And to live there as a naturalist, close to creatures of forest and woodland, and to become familiar with them and their changes over the seasons and the years. This chance was originally to study baboons, which became my life's work, but inevitably to become familiar also with the chimpanzees and their lives. Later came the responsibility of staying at the center on her behalf, while she was taken away by broader responsibilities to all corners of the globe.

Apart from the baboons and chimps, I also met, through her, many unusual and inspiring people, including visitors to the research station and researchers of every ilk. But the enduring privilege has been to live among the Tanzanians there, working closely with them, undivided by race or culture.

Jane has also provided guidance by example, especially in her commitment to promote what she cares about, whether it's the chimps at Gombe or environmental issues across the world. Her calm determination has been an object lesson. And in the same way, she practices what she preaches: makes few demands on her surroundings, eats little, seems hardly to sleep. Her room at the station is spartan, but she works there late into the night, writing and writing.

And she is a great letter writer, an unsung heroine of pen and paper. Her personal letters, handwritten and signed, supply her with a more meaningful way of reaching people than any stark printed e-mail. And there must be thousands of them, her personal messages distributed about the world!

In person, Jane is a great inspirer. When she was at Gombe in the '70s, she stimulated us greatly, talking with each student to offer guidance and new approaches, so much so that we would leave those meetings fairly buzzing with ideas, only later realizing we had to calm down, as we could not hope to do everything. And her vision from Gombe is also inspiring: that we can see the whole array of chimpanzees and other primates and all other animals as a continuum of life to pinpoint our place in the universe. That simple truth so clearly demonstrated has affected me as it has affected all who have heard and absorbed it.

But perhaps my greatest personal lesson has been to trust animals. She knows that there is usually nothing to fear from animals doing what they need to do, if you allow them to do it. They seldom have malice. If you remain calm, they remain calm. You gain nothing by panicking. And this is how she is with all animals. She trusts them. When I first saw Jane walking calmly through the middle of a baboon fight, it was an inspiring sight indeed—our primate unity demonstrated. As she talks, so she walks. So let us take that lesson from her and carry it with us.

DAVID ANTHONY COLLINS has studied baboons since 1972 at Gombe, where he is currently director of baboon research. He has done interim studies on other species in Ruaha, Serengeti, and Mahale.

The Six Degrees of Jane Goodall

MICHAEL A. HUFFMAN

Dear Jane,

The six-degrees-of-separation concept suggests that any two people on the planet are six or fewer acquaintance-links apart. No doubt this applies to you, Jane, as you have connected with so many of us around the world:

people who have in common a curiosity for all things living. Unique to you, perhaps, is that this network of connections built on friendships, professional and personal, with a common passion for nature, unites not only humans from every walk of life but also the animals we study and protect. From your very humble and unassuming character has sprung a powerful force for the change we all want to see.

I owe my first strong attachment to chimpanzees to my mother, who, starting when I was three years old, read me *The Adventures of Curious George*, and who gave me a life-size infant chimpanzee doll whose rubbery ears I still remember chewing on. But you were the nurturing force in my academic and moral development as a scientist. I am happy and humbled to have you as a friend and a valued mentor from my earliest days in primatology. Like many in my generation, growing up in the '6os and '7os, I was inspired by your discoveries as portrayed in *National Geographic*. These articles put a face and a concrete possibility to the dream of a three-year-old from Denver, Colorado, who promised his mother that one day he would "go to Africa and live with chimpanzees like Curious George."

Our close mutual friend and colleague, my graduate advisor at Kyoto University, the late Junichiro Itani, provided me with the unexpected opportunity to introduce myself to you at Aqua Lodge, Kigoma, in the summer of 1985. The realization of my childhood dream and the start of a successful career in chimpanzee research began that day, and you were there to share it with me. A common trait shared by both you and Itani sensei is your humanity and ability to interact with everyone you meet as equals, whether the person happens to be a humble villager, a naïve young graduate student, or a world leader of great influence. Few scientists were as gracious, unassuming, and open with their time and knowledge as you were with me during many stages of my career, and I greatly appreciate and admire you for that. You and Itani sensei have been my templates of what a scientist should be: humble, nurturing, sharing, and always enthusiastic.

MICHAEL A. HUFFMAN is associate professor in the Department of Ecology and Social Behavior at Kyoto University's Primate Research Institute. He conducts research widely across Africa and Asia.

It Started with a Letter

CRAIG STANFORD

I was living in a dilapidated hut in a rice paddy in Bangladesh, concluding my doctoral field research on Asian monkeys and seeking a new project to undertake after my PhD was completed. I got the idea that I would send a letter (actually a flimsy aerogram in the days before e-mail) to the most renowned scientist I could imagine, boldly looking for an invitation to collaborate. It was a message in a bottle mailed from a small village in Asia to a strange address in Dar es Salaam, Tanzania. I proposed to study the relationship between Dr. Goodall's famed chimpanzees and the red colobus monkeys they so eagerly hunt and eat. It would be a predator-prey study.

Several months later, when I arrived back at the University of California in Berkeley, I found a response from Jane in my mailbox. She invited me to work at Gombe, pending research clearance—not easily obtained in the late 1980s—and sufficient research funding. She also wanted to meet me, which happened some months later at the home of Geza Teleki in Washington, DC. The permits and funding took a year to arrange, and soon after that, I began my work in perhaps the most amazing and hallowed research site in the world of animal behavior study.

Through the early and mid-1990s, I commuted between Los Angeles and Gombe, sometimes bringing my family. Jane would periodically come out to Gombe herself, bringing a long list of chores and a desire to have some time alone in the forest, which we all respected. But during our time together watching the chimps, I was amazed at her sharp eyes and powers of observation of the tiniest details of her subjects' social life. She casually pointed out details of chimpanzee social behavior that I had routinely missed, even after months in the field. While I've since moved on to other projects and places, the privilege of sitting with Gombe's chimpanzees, all of us on a grassy bluff overlooking Lake Tanganyika, remains the high point of my field research career.

My professional connection to Jane and her causes extends over twenty years now. And while her impact on my life has been mainly professional, it has deeply influenced my personal life too. My wife, Erin, had worked as a volunteer for Jane in Gombe in the 1970s. My daughter, Gaelen, spent time at Gombe as a toddler, and over the years Gombe and Jane have been part of our family lore and shared memories. Her animal welfare causes and her veganism have been inspirations to us. Those of us who have been associated with Jane over the years carry on her message as best we can, and it never fails to astound me how global the reach of that message has been, from elegant dinner parties in Beverly Hills to the tiniest villages in Africa. What began for me as a coveted research opportunity with a renowned scientist has become far more than that.

CRAIG STANFORD, professor of biological sciences and codirector of the Jane Goodall Research Center at the University of Southern California, studied chimpanzees and colobus monkeys at Gombe in the 1990s. His most recent book is *Planet without Apes*.

Seeds of Hope in South America

PAULA GONZALEZ CICCIA

When I was a child, I was sure I wanted to help animals. Dr. Jane showed me that my dream could come true.

When I was ten years old, I became a vegetarian, and then, some years later, I decided to study biology. I learned many things about animals in studying biology, and I fell in love with primates, particularly chimpanzees and orangutans. I also read a lot about Jane Goodall and thus discovered her amazing life. And, of course, she inspired me. I remember my surprise when I realized that both of us were born on April 3, and I really wanted to meet her.

I finished my education and began working in wildlife conservation when something unexpected happened. I was chosen to participate in the JGI Global Youth Summit of 2008. That was an amazing experience, not only because I was able to meet Jane but also because I discovered the Jane Goodall Institute family around the world. Two years later, I started Roots & Shoots in Argentina, and today I have the great honor of being director of the Jane Goodall Institute in my country. JGI is growing, and now Latin America is part of it. The South American countries have incredible ecosystems with a great biodiversity—not only plants and animals but also the indigenous peoples who live close to nature—and we must conserve it all. People are inspired by Jane. Anywhere in the world, she reminds people of their need to connect with nature, and she sows seeds of hope. This year she did it in the Argentinean Patagonia too.

Jane is an incredible person—a leader and friend. I love her, and I am very grateful to have met her and have the opportunity to learn from her every day.

PAULA GONZALEZ CICCIA is director of the Jane Goodall Institute in Argentina.

Jane on Collaboration

POLLY CEVALLOS

Jane's personal philosophy is that the survival of chimpanzees or humans depends upon the collaboration of all people. This has become an everlasting mantra in my life.

No better example of this is how JGI works in Australia. Our programs are run by the most dedicated staff, and they include everyone when it comes to making decisions that affect so many others. Whether working on conservation action plans or making the required sustainable changes within a culture, we work within the communities, with their elders and their governments. We include all others who work within these areas—all other NGOs, zoos, or agencies under the global network of the International Union for Conservation of Nature (IUCN). We are part of a great big environmental family working together to ensure the survival of communities, environments, and all the beings who share this world.

This is a great template for us to aspire to and follow, and this is one of the many legacies that Jane will always be remembered for. Her inspirational story is one of adaptation, resilience, hope, courage, and passion. And her perseverance in the face of great opposition and the seemingly impossible has paid off. She is a guiding light for all of us to follow.

Jane has infused her passion and collaborative ethos within our family. My husband, Mark Richardson, is on the Australian board. Without him, JGI Australia would not be where it is today. And both our daughters are now following their passion with determination, working to save Australian marine parks and create change through music.

POLLY CEVALLOS founded the Jane Goodall Institute in Australia in 2006 with a small group of passionate people and was the CEO for five years.

Not What She Has Done

PETER L. BIRO

It is not what Jane has done or discovered in the forest but who she has been and how she has conducted herself that have impressed and influenced me in a profound and salutary fashion. I don't want to downplay the significance of Jane's research and her contribution to primatology, but her observations have always extended beyond the edge of the forest to include, as part of an organic, indivisible whole, the human community and civil society. The interdisciplinary quality of Jane's worldview—her methodology, observations, and prescriptions—has helped to validate and shape the way that I approach my own life and work.

Several years ago the filmmaker and organic farmer Camelia Frieberg and I cofounded Pollination Project, a social enterprise based on the south shore of Nova Scotia dedicated to exploring the connections between healthy food, artistic expression, mindful practices, and social justice. We were particularly inspired by the breadth and scope of Jane's work. We knew that her interdisciplinary worldview was enlightened and that, in resisting the modern cult of expertise and of disciplinary compartmentalization, it offered a way for each of us, specialists and generalists, experts and laypeople alike, to wake up each day empowered with the belief that we each could make a positive difference in the world.

I cannot write about Jane without referring to the way in which her extreme generosity and magnanimity intersect with a tireless devotion to her causes and principles. Jane has always been loyal and kind to her friends. But she has been equally generous—with time, advice, and allegiance—to those strangers she considers fellow travelers: people and organizations dedicated to furthering a mission she believes in.

And the camp of "fellow travelers" is, for Jane, a very large one. She is neither a snob nor an elitist (she has been known to drink Johnnie Walker Red Label . . . *Red* Label, for goodness sake!), and the community of fellow travelers includes all of nature's creatures and, indeed, even those of her opponents and adversaries she believes to be susceptible of changing their minds or capable of changing hers. She is one of my greatest heroes and teachers. I have learned to be a better advocate, listener, activist, and friend by paying attention to Jane's own style of engaging with others. Her willingness to commune with the opposition rather than merely preach to the converted has not only endeared her to so many; it has, more impressively, promoted a message of constructive engagement with the world. Nothing expresses this more poignantly than her famous statement "Change happens by listening and then starting a dialogue with the people who are doing something you don't believe is right." How blessed I feel to have learned this from her.

PETER L. BIRO, a Canadian lawyer and businessman, is chair of the Jane Goodall Institute Global, a director of the Jane Goodall Institute of Canada, president and CEO of Newcon Optik, and cofounder of Pollination Project.

Just Like David Greybeard

FEDERICO BOGDANOWICZ

It was 2007. I had recently visited a chimpanzee rescue center and learned about the plight of primates exploited in show business. I remember seeing an adult chimp who had spent most of his life in a tiny cage. His body was not fully developed, and his back was impossibly crooked. I looked into his brown eyes and saw pain, anger, and sadness. Maybe that was reflected in my eyes, too. I felt ashamed of my own species. I decided to do something, I did not know what, but I was tired of complaining and then doing nothing.

Soon afterward, I had the chance to attend a lecture in Barcelona by Dr. Jane Goodall. It was absolutely magical: the insight of her speech, showing us that everyone can make a difference; her wise words, not learned from a book but backed up by decades of hard work and tireless activism. The experience was one of the most inspiring moments of my life. At the end, I waited in line just to shake her hand in silence, to express my gratitude for all she had done and all the things she had renounced in order to make the world a better place. She smiled humbly

and said, in response to my silence, "Just like David Greybeard," as she
shook my hand. David Greybeard was the chimp who introduced her to
the fascinating world of wild chimpanzees in Gombe. He was also the
protagonist of many special moments, such as when he waited for her as
she pushed her way through the tangled vegetation. They both sat down,
side by side, and then Jane held out a red palm nut to thank him—but
he turned his face away. She held her hand closer, and then he looked
directly into her eyes. He reached out and took the nut. He didn't want
it. He dropped it. But at the same time, he very gently squeezed Jane's
fingers, which is how one chimp reassures another.

Just like David Greybeard with the nut, Jane did not seek my gratitude and admiration, but she gently squeezed my hand, meaning that she
appreciated it. Then I understood that being grateful is not enough. At
seventy-one, she was traveling 300 days a year around the world not to
be thanked by us but rather to help us realize that we need to take action.

I had entered the conference a nihilist. I walked out an activist, willing to make a difference no matter how small. I joined the Jane Goodall
Institute as a volunteer and became her interpreter in Spain, enjoying
more opportunities to listen to and learn from this fantastic human being.
Inspired by her work, I quit my job and decided to devote my time to
the Jane Goodall Institute, to primates and biodiversity. I became the
cocreator and manager of an environmental education program called
Biodiverciudad (Biodiversity), aimed at exploring the fabulous treasure of
biodiversity in our cities. Now, at the JGI in Spain, I am privileged to
collaborate with chimpanzee rescue, conservation, and research projects
in Africa. In a magical turn of events, I get to organize Jane's conferences in Spain to help spread her message to others. I have been extremely
fortunate to meet Jane, to learn from her, to become her friend. She has

made such a huge difference in my life, more than she will ever know. Just as David Greybeard did for her, Jane has introduced me to an utterly new and fascinating world.

FEDERICO BOGDANOWICZ, anthropologist and primatologist, is the executive director of the Jane Goodall Institute in Spain and runs its Roots & Shoots program.

A Meeting in Gombe

FERRAN GUALLAR

I am probably among the least orthodox economists I have ever known. Actually, I hate economists. Since my childhood I had always wanted to become a biologist. How did I end up being an economist? Long story. No need for details. After a few jobs (guitar teacher, music school administrator, export manager in the Middle East and Magreb, and so on), I became a marketing specialist at Microsoft. Yes.

Five years later, I realized I needed something else in my life, so I asked for a leave of absence. The sabbatical became a five-year break, and I never went back to that job. For the first two years I traveled the world without coming back home. I went everywhere, including places like the northwest frontier of Pakistan, Syria, Iran, and Sudan. (Note for the CIA: I also went to other countries that are *not* in the Axis of Evil). I wanted to learn firsthand what the media and others filter and interpret for us every day, the prejudices and self-interested manipulations that infect our values and views on the world. Since I knew it would be difficult to travel like that for a long time (I lived on almost nothing during this journey), I put together a project called School of the World, which filmed and edited short videos for schools located in small, isolated villages. At the same time, the students and teachers in these schools would share things they knew with Spanish students and teachers via my web page.

When I arrived in Tanzania, traveling overland from Southeast Asia, I had in mind two or three ideas for brief videos. One of them would be an interview with Jane Goodall, whom I had come to know from documentaries and also, especially, from a friend who was a Goodall fan. I hadn't read any of her books, so I was almost a blank sheet on which she might leave her imprint.

I arrived at Gombe. Always an optimist, I waited for her to arrive. One tiny detail I didn't know at the time was that Jane spends very little time in Gombe, since she had left field research many years earlier. I waited there for about ten days, pestering the photographer there, Bill Wallauer, his wife, Mtiti, and others, asking them repeatedly when Jane was going to arrive. I was naïve but also lucky. She arrived!

I still remember that moment: Jane disembarking onto the beach at Gombe. She had an eye problem, but she was really nice to me. She patiently gave the interview, talking a lot about our educational projects: mine on cultural and natural diversity, hers with something called Roots & Shoots. She said I was an active young man and that the JGI needed someone to open and run a Jane Goodall Institute in Spain.

We met again in 2006, in Spain, after the end of my world tour. That second meeting sealed my fate. I raised the funds for JGI Spain immediately. I specialized in protected areas management, and I am currently working in the field, running a program in West Africa, where we have created a protected area dedicated to chimp conservation. We have also built a research station, and we teach people in local communities about resource management, ecotourism, and sustainable agriculture. I hope these contributions will protect chimpanzees from extinction. That's how Jane changed my life.

FERRAN GUALLAR has been leading JGI Spain's West African programs since 2009. Trained as an economist specializing in protected areas management, he is also a decent guitar player.

Every Individual Matters

PETER APELL

"Every individual matters. Every individual has a role to play. Every individual makes a difference." Working for years as a veterinarian at the Jane Goodall Institute has taught me that these three declarations, the maxim of the institution, are more than a motivational trinity. When I first took them in, though, I wondered whether much substance lay beneath their inspirational aspect.

We have five thousand chimpanzees in the wild in Uganda and an estimated 150,000 across Africa. Some of them are in protected areas, but most are outside that supposedly safe haven. How, I kept asking myself, are we to take care of each individual among these chimpanzees? Once I had posed the question and begun to consider it, I felt daunted by the scale of the task it revealed—and also motivated by the scale of success it promised. This captures Jane's mastery: the use of simple, sometimes subtle, but often powerful expressions to motivate action.

Not long ago, it was widely believed, and still is in some circles of the chimpanzee conservation fraternity, that anesthetic immobilization of wild chimpanzees in need of medical care is a greater risk than letting nature take its course. This is because of the tendency of chimpanzees to climb trees when startled by the impact of the projectile used to deliver the anesthetic. When the anesthesia actually arrives, they will lose all motor control and can fall from a high perch to their death below! That was the thinking. On the other hand, abandoning human intervention altogether would consign chimpanzees to some grim probabilities of survival after they've suffered grave injury, especially given the increasing frequency of such injuries. Around one-quarter of the chimpanzees from habituated tourism and research groups in Uganda have injuries related to snares or jaw-traps, and many have died. Emotionally, I found it hard to stand by and watch passively as individual chimpanzees were maimed or killed by jaw-traps and snares. More practically, though, I began to understand that much of the chimp population in Uganda is fragmented into small groups, which means that losing one individual, especially a female, could further imperil their survival and that of the species.

"Every individual matters. Every individual has a role to play. Every individual makes a difference." The logic of this maxim has pushed me to think beyond the risk of darting the chimpanzees to the risk of not darting them. In fact, the latter is a more frightening proposition. Today, seven years after I took inspiration from that unassuming statement, we have successfully immobilized over thirty chimpanzees in the wild with a 100 percent success rate: saving limbs, saving lives, and hopefully saving populations.

PETER APELL works as a veterinarian with JGI Uganda.

One Person Can Make a Difference

DONALD R. KENDALL

I met Jane through the Houston Zoo and was fortunate enough to have her stay at our home. After a full day of meetings and presentations, she and I relaxed outside by our pool, talking. I learned about her interest in all living things and her intellectual curiosity from a young age. She told me about her mother's gentle way of dealing with this exceptional daughter: "Don't you think those worms under your pillow will be better outside?" I was impressed by her mother's patience when Jane went missing for hours, hiding in the henhouse and trying to find out where eggs came from. And I was fascinated by the fact that Jane, as a young female researcher, was not permitted to travel to Gombe on her own, so her mother went with her.

Jane and I went back indoors. Sometime later I heard a loud crash from her room. The next morning, I found out that the bed had broken, and so she had slept on a slanted mattress all night long. Her gracious response: "It was still better than many nights I spent in the field."

I was lucky enough to spend a few days in Gombe with Jane and found it amazing to hike the same trails she had hiked when she first arrived there in 1960. I was also delighted and impressed to see the Jane Goodall Institute projects at work in the villages surrounding Gombe and to witness the impact they are having on the lives of the local people. But one of my best memories from that time comes from sitting on the beach at Gombe watching the sun set while Dr. Anthony Collins (baboon researcher and all-around problem solver) groomed Jane just like the chimpanzees groom each other.

Jane's seemingly endless intellectual curiosity and her remarkable optimism and faith in humanity and the world have had a big impact on my
life. She clearly believes and demonstrates that one person can make a
difference.

DONALD R. KENDALL is the founding managing director of Kenmont
Solutions and president and CEO of Blue Earth Capital, Inc. He is the vice chair
and was until recently cochair of the Jane Goodall Institute.

Travels with Jane

DILYS MACKINNON

I remember clearly buying my first copy of *National Geographic* in 1965,
while I was working for UNICEF in New York, because of the picture of
Jane on the front cover. I had never heard of this young English girl doing
pioneering work on chimpanzees in Tanzania. I was full of admiration for
her spirit of adventure and dedication, and I thought, How exciting and
how brave of her to be studying chimpanzees alone in the jungle.

About twenty years later, I was working for a nonprofit procurement
company in the UK supplying goods to aid and development projects
in parts of East Africa. I was surprised and delighted to discover that a
Norwegian friend, the director of an aid project in Tanzania, had met
Jane in Dar es Salaam. She had mentioned to him that she was finding it
impossible to locate spare parts for her twenty-year-old car and was therefore unable to use it. He suggested she contact us and have the spare parts
shipped out with his next consignment. We were able to help, and the
next time Jane was in Bournemouth, she and her mother, Vanne, came

along to our offices at Southampton Airport. That was the beginning of my long and inspiring friendship with both Vanne and Jane.

Jane wanted to set up an institute in the UK, and in 1989, I offered to get it going on a voluntary basis, thinking it would not take much time. How wrong I was! Within a couple of years I was working full time at the Jane Goodall Institute, particularly involved with our projects in Africa, and organizing Jane's schedule outside the United States.

From then on I traveled with Jane at least once a year to projects in Tanzania, Kenya, Uganda, Burundi, and Congo-Brazzaville. For me these were fascinating, sometimes alarming, often frustrating, but above all, educational and rewarding visits. I learned to drink whiskey, which is essential for anyone traveling with Jane, and to exist on much less food than I was used to, as sustenance does come low on Jane's list of priorities. Flights across Tanzania, from Dar at the edge of the Indian Ocean to Kigoma at the edge of Lake Tanganyika, were always a stimulating experience, and our visits to Congo-Brazzaville were inevitably challenging. The chimpanzee sanctuary there grew faster than any other, mainly because the illegal bushmeat trade in that area was creating so many baby orphans, and yet it was an amazingly expensive country. I acted as Jane's French interpreter, and we constantly shuttled between the coast and the capital, trying to sort out the formidable amounts of red tape.

But staying in Jane's home in Dar es Salaam was a real adventure in itself. When I first went there, a tree was poking through the roof, the windows couldn't be closed even in a gale or torrential rain, the mosquito netting was shot, and the water and electricity were unreliable. Meanwhile, an interesting variety of people lived there or were passing through. It was also the only house along the seafront without an eight-foot-high electric security fence to keep out intruders, and for protection, Jane depended on an ancient night watchman armed with a bow and arrow! Jane, in fact, has never spent money on herself or craved creature comforts, and I think she was unconcerned about any of these problems. Any money she is able to raise has always gone into projects to help those in need, human or animal.

In the midst of her crazy schedule, Jane writes hundreds of letters to friends, admirers, and others who rely on her for emotional support. I have never sat on a plane with her when she hasn't had a stack of cards and writing paper, and by the end, there is always a mound of letters to be stamped and posted. She has been a huge inspiration to many people and still refuses to slow down. Clearly she will never retire, and the world is a better place for all that she is doing and has done. I think of her as a true friend and am grateful for all the fun and rewarding times we have had together, particularly traveling in Africa.

DILYS MACKINNON held a variety of jobs while her children were growing up. She was senior buyer for Lifeline (supplying development projects in Africa) in 1988 and 1989, and executive director of the Jane Goodall Institute UK from 1989 to 2003.

A Calm Spirit

CLAIRE QUARENDON

I started working for the Jane Goodall Institute UK in 2001. On meeting Jane for the first time, I noticed that she has an amazing serenity about her. I have been to many of her lectures. Each time I hear her talk, I fall totally under her spell. It feels like everything and everyone around her disappears, and I am hypnotized by her words.

Jane was incredibly supportive when I lost my father in 2007, and her words during that very difficult time still mean a lot to me.

CLAIRE QUARENDON started working for the Jane Goodall Institute UK in 2001 and is now the office manager, working closely with Jane when Jane is in the United Kingdom.

You Encouraged Me

GUDRUN SCHINDLER-RAINBAUER

Dear Jane,

I was studying biology when I met you for the first time in Vienna, twenty years ago. I was also working as a campaigner for another NGO, and I organized—together with JGI Austria—the first Peace Day event at the UN office in Vienna. Some months later, I was asked if I would like to work at the Jane Goodall Institute in Austria.

My little Jakob was already two years old, and my husband, Michael, hadn't yet finished his studies. So I was not sure. But Michael encouraged me. My dream had always been to do useful work for children and for Africa, and Michael told me that I should make my dream a reality. So I gave up a full-paid job and changed to a full-day job. But I never have regretted it. *Never!*

During the last seven years I've worked with you, I have so often heard and read your story about what your mother, Vanne, told you: "We can make our dreams a reality if we work hard and believe in ourselves." Vanne encouraged you always, and she taught you never to give up. That was one of the most important things I learned from you: not to give up.

So Vanne gave it to you, you gave it to me, and now I am giving it to my three children: Jakob, Jonas, and Wenzel. I am happy and deeply grateful for what I've learned from you. Wherever you are, Jane, I want to be there for you.

GUDRUN SCHINDLER-RAINBAUER, zoologist and ecologist, studied at the University of Vienna, worked with children in the national parks of Austria, and is executive director of the JGI Austria.

The Spirit of Jane

PHEE BOON KANG

I met Jane after her speech at Taipei American School in the fall of 1996, during her first visit to Taiwan. I had found myself incredibly moved by her touching stories about the chimpanzees she studied, learned from, and devoted her entire life to.

After her speech and before she was ushered into a room full of students, I shared with Jane my desire to help, in spite of my total lack of knowledge or experience with animal welfare and conservation. She called me a few days later, kicking off a seventeen-year journey for me that continues today. The Jane Goodall Institute in Taiwan was launched after that first phone call. Then, in 1999, I flew to Paris to meet her and David Shear, among other helpers, to deliberate the need to form a global body that would support the Institute's growing number of chapters around the world. JGI Global finally became a reality in the summer of 2013.

Starting with that speech at that school in the fall of 1996, I have found myself comparing Jane to the traditional Chinese concept of a living Guanyin, an enlightened Buddha revered for providing assistance to everyday folks in distress. Guanyin is the Chinese rendition of a female Buddhist bodhisattva, whose hallmark is compassion and empathy for the suffering multitudes. (This is believed to have evolved from the Indian concept of Avalokitesvara.) Like a Guanyin, Jane has a special message that resonates easily with her diverse audience. She is an incredibly articulate storyteller who routinely captivates audiences with her unusual serenity. Of course, Jane's accomplishments go far beyond experiencing compassion and into actual action. Hers is not a reserved kind of Buddhist wisdom, reflecting on the ephemeral nature of life. Jane's mission is distinctively an activist one, built around a call for optimism and the harnessing of the indomitable human willingness for change, invention, and righting wrongs.

Jane is spontaneous, especially when she is in her element, and she comes across as delightfully youthful when she is moved, as when she took part in the annual animal parades held in recent years in Taipei and Hsinchu, the Silicon Valley of Taiwan.

Jane's incredible attention to the little things inspires me every day not to lose track of the important details in my own life. Her powers of observation surely feed her holistic approach to guarding nature and wildlife, caring for both animals and humans alike, all while maintaining an indefatigable optimism. It has been a privilege for me to have accompanied Jane in her awesome journey, to make the world a better place for all.

PHEE BOON KANG is the president of Boon Associates, a director at Citibank Japan, a founder and chair emeritus of both JGI Global and JGI Taiwan, and a trustee at Beloit College.

TACARE

GEORGE STRUNDEN

When a friend mentioned I should give Jane Goodall a call because her Institute was urgently looking for a project director in Tanzania, I had no idea what I was getting myself into. At that time I was working with the German Development Service not far from Gombe National Park, and my contract was about to end. But after a few phone calls and an interview, I was offered the job and ended up working for the Institute for the next eighteen years.

Jane and the JGI UK director Dilys McKinnon were the kindest bosses you can imagine. I was given the task of developing a way to halt and possibly reverse the relentless deforestation and degradation of the landscape surrounding Gombe. But what was initially imagined to be a treeplanting project evolved into a multisector rural development intervention that linked biodiversity objectives with the development aspirations of the local people.

First we had to gain the trust of sometimes-hostile villagers and a local government that wanted to see the Gombe National Park dissolved and the land redistributed to the neighboring communities. After assembling a dedicated and capable team of Tanzanian experts, we all lived for weeks at a time in the villages around Gombe. In village after village we sat in seemingly endless meetings with elders and community leaders, listening and discussing causes of land degradation. In the end, we jointly developed a specific action plan for each village designed to reverse the land degradation. That's how the TACARE project was established.

TACARE (pronounced Take Care) is an acronym for the Lake

Tanganyika Catchment Area Reforestation and Education project. After starting with the tree planting and erosion control, we moved on to facilitate a comprehensive plan for land use that involved the government at several levels. Today you can actually see how the landscape around Gombe has started to regain its green tree cover. And if you look a little more closely, you will recognize that the TACARE project has not only halted the land degradation around the park, but it has also, in many other ways, improved the lives of many thousands of the rural poor who happen to live on the edges of chimpanzee habitat in that part of the world.

Building on the successes of TACARE, we engaged villagers not merely around Gombe but also those living all the way to the Masito-Ugalla ecosystem in the south, changing attitudes toward the conservation of nature and especially of chimpanzees. Through a participatory process, we generated a lasting constructive foundation on which development and conservation efforts thrive. And now, with a team of driven and gifted individuals, we have begun building similar programs in Uganda and the two Congos.

The years I spent starting and growing the TACARE project were the most rewarding of my life, and I can look back on them with the fondest memories. Working with Jane was invigorating, inspiring, and highly motivating. And the truly international nature of the Institute made it a rewarding environment where I was continuously exposed to the most interesting people from all over the world. In a world filled with despair and cruelty, Jane's kindness, patience, and wisdom remain an inspiration.

GEORGE STRUNDEN, vice president of the Jane Goodall Institute's Africa Program, created the TACARE community-based conservation project.

Who Is Jane Goodall?

MARY LEWIS

In 1990, my "normal" life took a 180-degree turn: from corporate to chaotic. As senior manager in government and public affairs for Conoco UK, and as chair of the safety steering committee, I was attending a conference in Arizona to receive an award for corporate safety. Meanwhile, the president of Conoco, Inc., Dino Nicandros, had invited someone named Jane Goodall to lunch in order to discuss chimpanzees. At the time I was also working on arrangements for a royal banquet in Houston during British week, and—save for a childhood visit to Dudley Zoo in the 1950s where the chimps were dressed up like people—I knew nothing about chimpanzees. I knew even less about Jane Goodall. Who was she? Another complete mystery: what was Conoco, an international petroleum company, doing with chimpanzees?

But I listened to what Jane Goodall had to say. It turned out that Conoco Congo was exploring for oil on the western edge of Central Africa and had agreed to help the Jane Goodall Institute construct a sanctuary to house an increasing number of chimpanzee orphans near an area where they had been drilling. And so I met Jane at that conference—and soon Conoco was hosting lunches, dinners, and even JGI board meetings in London. Conoco Chairman Mike Stinson had by then joined the board of JGI UK, and, before I knew it, I was helping ship a container load of fencing and veterinary supplies to Congo-Brazzaville!

For me, it was the start of a global adventure. Because I was considered to be someone with organizational skills, I became part of Conoco's commitment to Jane and the Jane Goodall Institute. I spent many hours with Jane's mother, Vanne, and her friend, Genie di san Faustino, at the

Madison Hotel in Washington, DC, while we were there to see Jane receive the Hubbard Medal from the National Geographic. Genie (the founding president of the JGI USA board) felt that Jane "needed help"—and so began my new life in the form of a twenty-one-day U.S. tour that Genie funded. But who was this mysterious Jane Goodall? The first hour of the first day on the road began to unravel the mystery—starting with the midnight requests for autographs, photographs, or books to be signed that continues daily wherever Jane is in the world.

It has been and continues to be a long and glorious road. Since the 1990s, that road has gone to Ridgefield, Connecticut, and Washington, DC; to Montana, Nebraska, and Wyoming; from Lake Louise to Sydney; Costa Rica to the Serengeti; Johannesburg to Delhi; to Munich, Monaco, Mumbai, and Manaus; and to Cambodia and Cambridge. To reach those countless cities in many countries, there were too many flights, dozens of trains, and strange car journeys. And then there is Mr. H and his continual ability to vanish.

But there have been the magical oases—the base camps made up of friends that often involve food. But not just any food: a picnic in Vermont of home-grown tomatoes and organic cheese; Chinese and Indian takeout at ChimpanZoo in New York; curled cheeses in hot hotel rooms in Boston (while countless crane prints were signed and numbered on the floor); the desperate search for something that was not meat in a hotel overlooking the stinking stockyards in Lubbock, Texas, around the time *Harvest for Hope* was published; the melted Twix at midnight or even for lunch; and the candlelit feasts at No. 8 for assorted travelers and various film crews and all their equipment.

And there are the moments that Hollywood can only dream about: the small child, waiting outside in the pouring rain, clutching a plastic bag of coins to give to Jane; being locked backstage with skeleton costumes and wigs in Busch Gardens; the extraordinary moment when Chimpanzee Wounda emerged into her new island home at Tchimpounga Chimpanzee Rehabilitation Center and hugged Jane; the freak storm that trapped us for two days in Spearfish Canyon with impassable banks of snow and just the right group of people, the perfect circumstance for bringing Roots & Shoots to more Native American communities; the ice storms in Atlanta; and then the day trapped in the Grolimonds' house with a huge tree full of feeding birds outside in the thickest snow.

And so many lives altered. People trapped in basements under gunfire in Sarajevo reading *In the Shadow of Man.* The college student hitchhiking from Chicago to Milwaukee in the snow, seeking a ticket for the lecture . . . who then became an R&S intern in Africa. Those who brought up their children based on Jane's experiences with chimpanzees and her son, Grub. The countless others who changed direction to follow their dreams. The veterinarians who chose their field because of her. The field scientists studying lemurs or toads or ants because of her. The children who appear with precious letters she once wrote from Gombe to their parents or grandparents. The gentleness in violent times during the 9/11 lockdown in New York City; the gathering of friends and Muslim visitors while Yasmine Delawari's father shared his wisdom by phone from LA; arriving in Colorado to the news of the Columbine shooting and Jane giving her lecture and starting the healing process for many shocked hearts. The vast cobweb that R&S has become, growing so rapidly all over the JGI world. The amazing volunteers and staff and their tireless efforts to keep things going, and the wonderful friendships and warmth of the JGI global family. The endless e-mail correspondence that begins, "I met Jane in an airport"—or "on a train" or "in a bus station." The passionate young people wanting to work with animals; the disillusioned teenagers needing and finding a sense of purpose; the sick being nurtured with spoken or written words.

It doesn't seem to end. There are a thousand facets to the diamond that is Jane. I can only begin to identify the sparkle of a few.

After a country upbringing surrounded by animals, followed by twenty-five years working in the oil and gas industry, MARY LEWIS became involved with the Jane Goodall Institute in 1990 and has worked since then to support Jane in her many programs around the world.

JANE AS PARTNER

Jane has often partnered with others in causes that may at first have seemed outside the scope of her core interests and reputation. In fact, there was a time when Jane's core interests did not include chimpanzee conservation or welfare. She was first a pioneering scientist trained in ethology and studying chimpanzee behavior in the field. That changed in 1986 as she reached some of her goals as a scientist and paused to look beyond the world of Gombe. That pause, that looking beyond, resulted in a sudden, inspired conversion. Jane became aware of the enormous conservation crisis threatening chimpanzees across Africa. At the same time, she started to recognize the unhappy and often abusive conditions for chimpanzees held in captivity outside Africa. And she resolved to act.

Among the worst of abusive conditions could be found inside an American biomedical laboratory known as Sema, Inc., which was located in a suburban shopping mall in Rockville, Maryland. Jane became aware of the horrific conditions for caged primates (many of them chimpanzees) at Sema by watching a videotape sent to her by the animal rights organization People for the Ethical Treatment of Animals (PETA). She supported the PETA campaign to free the Sema primates, and she contributed to it with her expert opinion on the evils of that particular laboratory. She then opened her own campaign to change Sema and similar laboratories by writing an open letter to the *New York Times*. That was followed by meetings with people from the laboratory along with high-ranking officials from the lab's funding source, the U.S. National Institutes of Health (NIH); conferences and discussions with laboratory scientists and directors across the country and in Europe; and some persistent lobbying of influential politicians in Washington.

Shamed by Jane's public charges and critical follow-through, the Sema management changed the laboratory's name and over time made significant improvements in the architecture and protocol. It was a small battle partially won, although as PETA president and founder Ingrid Newkirk writes, it was just the start. The larger campaign, involving new laws and new attitudes—such as the understanding that "chimpanzees are someone not something"—has taken place over the last two to three decades. Jane and her friends, colleagues, and partners have succeeded to the point that the NIH, once the world's largest holder of captive chimps, recently announced that 310 of its 360 chimpanzees still in cages would soon be freed.

But freed under what conditions? That was always the question. Over time, the answer has been provided by a number of dedicated people who sometimes turned to Jane for advice and help. Tony Smith, president of the Fauna Foundation, describes Jane's partnership with that organization and her "unwavering support and encouragement" in the quest to make a home for fifteen chimp refugees from laboratories. Many other refugees from U.S. labs were taken in by another sanctuary, Save the Chimps, founded by Carole Noon. Philanthropic funding partner Jon Stryker refers to his own passion in protecting great apes in the third essay and in addition writes on behalf of the late Dr. Noon. Patti Ragan established a sanctuary for apes as well, a process she describes in "Jane and My Grub," and today the Center for Great Apes in Wauchula, Florida, provides a home for more than forty ape refugees from the entertainment industry. Jane has also visited and encouraged other people running other sanctuaries in the United States, such as Chimps Inc. in Oregon. Leslie Day, founder and president of Chimps Inc., writes of Jane's visit there in "A Soft-Spoken Woman."

During the late 1980s and early 1990s, European and Asian logging companies arrived in Central Africa with enough modern machinery to begin ripping their way into the sixty-five-million-year-old Congo Basin rain forests—and incidentally opening up the forests to a major secondary industry providing exotic meats to well-off consumers in the big cities. Ian Redmond, sent to Congo-Brazzaville to investigate and document the growing signs of this so-called bushmeat commerce, also documented the conditions for chimpanzees held in the Pointe Noire "zoo" and the growing numbers of bushmeat orphans—including ape infants whose mothers had been killed by commercial meat hunters. Redmond tells the story of his discoveries and Jane's early partnerships in Central Africa, which include the creation of JGI's Tchimpounga Chimpanzee Rehabilitation Center, now the biggest ape orphanage in Africa.

Still not fully recognized is the enormous public health cost of the bushmeat trade, particularly as it involves the killing, butchering, and eating of humanity's closest relatives. Virologist Beatrice H. Hahn did some of the original work documenting the origins of HIV-1 (the human virus that causes 99 percent of AIDS cases) in a nearly identical virus, known as SIVcpz, that is endemic among chimpanzees. In her essay, Hahn describes the partnership with Jane that has enabled her to test the Gombe chimpanzees for the presence of SIVcpz and to do the work that may one day, as she puts it, "drive SIVcpz in Gombe to extinction."

While Jane is strongly identified with chimpanzees and her pioneering studies of them, she is in fact a woman of diverse interests and talents, so we should not be surprised to learn that her partnerships have made her a defender of African Grey Parrots (according to parrot-language expert Irene Pepperberg), an ambassador on behalf of bears (writes Jill Robinson, founder of Animals Asia Foundation), a supporter and advisor on behalf of cougars (Cara Blessley Lowe, cofounder of the Cougar Fund), and a protector of wild camels (John Hare, founder of the Wild Camel Protection Foundation). More recently, she has taken up the cause of plants and the dangers of genetically modified foods—

and enlisted the partnership of writer Gail Hudson to collaborate on the book called *Seeds of Hope: Wisdom and Wonder from the World of Plants* (2014). Hudson describes some aspects of that partnership in her essay. Another partner in literary enterprise is Vivian B. Wheeler. As editor for Jane's scientific opus, *The Chimpanzees of Gombe* (1986), Wheeler left the comforts of Cambridge, Massachusetts, for the scary wilds of the African continent in order to confer with this peculiar woman who had written a very big book.

Jane is, to summarize, the "spark that rallies people" (in the words of Charles Knowles, founder of the Wildlife Conservation Network), and "a partner in this great cause of helping [all] animals" (according to Wayne Pacelle, president and CEO of the Humane Society of the United States).

—D. P.

Jane and the Sema Chimps

INGRID NEWKIRK

In January 2013, something momentous happened—something that People for the Ethical Treatment of Animals (PETA) had dreamed of since an incident almost thirty years earlier. What happened is that the National Institutes of Health (NIH) announced it was retiring 310 of the 360 chimpanzees still held for research. They were going to sanctuaries, and the rest will surely follow soon.

But it all really began in 1986, when four baby chimpanzees were removed under cover of night from Sema, an NIH-funded, infectious disease laboratory. The chimpanzee infants were spirited away by an animal liberation group called True Friends, and the videotape they took inside Sema showed adult chimpanzees living in refrigerator-like cages, rocking back and forth, banging their heads against the metal and Plexiglas walls, having gone mad from long-term and grossly inhumane confinement. Baby chimpanzees at Sema awaited the same fate.

The videotape shocked people, including Jane Goodall, who could now see the plight of involuntary experimental subjects who happen to be our closest living relatives. When distributing the videotapes of the bleak conditions in which the chimpanzees were housed, PETA coined the phrase "breaking the species barrier" to describe what needed to be done.

I met with Dr. Goodall. She had watched the tape with, as she put it, "shock and anger," asked informed questions, and decided to visit the facility to see for herself. She persuaded the laboratory director to allow her to visit. Regarding the tape and the subsequent visit, she wrote an open letter that was published in the *New York Times* and laid one of the first stepping stones that led finally to the 2013 NIH announcement.

Thank you, Jane, for opening people's eyes to the idea that a chimpanzee is some*one* not some*thing* and for helping us topple the first species barrier in a long waiting line.

INGRID NEWKIRK is the founder and president of People for the Ethical Treatment of Animals and the author of *Free the Animals! Making Kind Choices* and *The PETA Practical Guide to Animal Rights*.

Fifteen Chimpanzees

TONY SMITH

Seventeen years ago I was introduced to the important work of Jane Goodall by my dear friend and sister-in-law, Gloria Grow. Inspired by

Goodall's writings and tireless work with chimpanzees, Gloria had become determined to provide a home and lifelong, loving care for fifteen former subjects of biomedical research. The arrival of fifteen very special chimpanzees at their new home, what we called the Fauna Foundation, would forever change the course of my life and the lives of my family in an extremely positive way.

Jane's unwavering support and encouragement for Gloria's mission has been a source of great inspiration to me, and I have had the privilege of witnessing precious interactions between Jane and our extended family of chimpanzees during her many visits to Fauna. I have been inspired by those interactions and also by Jane's heartwarming stories that speak volumes of uncompromising compassion and conscious choices. Her support has strengthened my resolve to continue doing whatever I can to make this world a better place.

The universal message that Jane carries with her: "Each one of us matters, has a role to play, and makes a difference. Each one of us must take responsibility for our own lives, and above all, show respect and love for living things around us, especially each other." Her message of hope resonates strongly in my mind and has helped to reinforce my belief that all humans can learn to treat people and the other sentient creatures on this planet in the positive and compassionate manner that they deserve.

Jane's support has been instrumental in the international recognition that Fauna has achieved. Such recognition has allowed us, through the sad stories of our chimpanzee family, to garner the support that we need to accomplish our mission by working in partnership with others to ensure that we make the world a better place. I remain eternally grateful to my friend Jane for the inspiration, encouragement, and confidence she has given Gloria that, in turn, gives her the will to continue in this rewarding but difficult task.

TONY SMITH works in the aerospace industry and is president of Fauna Sanctuary, Inc. He serves on the advisory board of the Fauna Foundation, Canada's first and only chimpanzee sanctuary.

For Dr. Carole Noon

JON STRYKER

Dear Jane,

I was five years old in 1963 when I first saw your first National Geographic film. Thereafter, throughout my youth, I inhaled each of your books and articles. I knew each of the Gombe chimps by name and face and became familiar with their complex society. I covered my bedroom walls with pictures of monkeys and apes in a huge wall-to-wall collage. I dreamed of living in a tropical forest and helping apes just like you were doing. My fascination with chimps (and all primates) has never ceased and has greatly enriched my life. Your impact on the trajectory of my life continues to this day, and I feel I owe you so much gratitude. When people ask me how I became one of the world's largest funders of Great Ape sanctuaries, research, and conservation projects, the beginning of the story always starts with you!

If Carole were here today to share her thoughts I think she would want to tell the story about how she attended one of your lectures in Florida and how, in that one hour, the course of her life was changed forever. Carole realized there and then that her life's work was to become a primatologist and work to help chimpanzees. She would want to remind you of how encouraging you were, how you suggested she go to Africa to see the reality of chimps in the wild and to work at the Chimfunshi chimp sanctuary in Zambia, and how you got her to think about how she could help captive chimps back here in the States. I think she would want to tell you that Save the Chimps, the largest chimp sanctuary in the world, would never have happened without your help and advice.

And finally, I think she would want you to know how deeply she loved and admired you.

JON STRYKER is the founder and president of Arcus Foundation, which supports great ape conservation and social justice causes. The threatened colobine species *Rhinopithecus strykeri* is named after him.

Jane and My Grub

PATTI RAGAN

As one of the multitudes who had read *In the Shadow of Man*, I was thrilled when I first met Jane Goodall in 1983, at a three-day conference at Sweet Briar College. The special symposium sponsored by the National Geographic Society included *National Geographic* magazine's four "cover ladies"—Jane Goodall, Dian Fossey, Biruté Galdikas, and Penny Patterson—each of whom gave a presentation about her fieldwork. Given that I was already a great ape groupie, seeing those four ladies was a pivotal moment and a dream come true. I was actually meeting in person the amazing women I had read about!

The following year, I worked in Borneo for several months tracking orangutans with Dr. Galdikas before returning to my usual life in Miami, managing a family business. Five years later, because of my experience in Borneo, I was asked to temporarily provide care for an infant orangutan at a tourist attraction in Miami, and then, one year later, I was given the task of caring for an infant chimpanzee. Since the baby chimp was in my volunteer care for a few months, I was also given the job of naming him. Wanting to honor Jane Goodall, I named him Grub after her nickname for her son. I thought Grub would be sent to a zoo accredited by the Association of Zoos and Aquariums (AZA), but I soon learned that his owner planned to sell him to a Hollywood animal trainer.

Distressed at this possible future for precious Grub, I had a conversation with Jane—and for the first time talked about starting a sanctuary not only for Pongo, the orangutan I was caring for, but also for Grub. Jane patiently listened to my idea and cautioned me about the difficulties of starting such a venture, given the permanent commitment and financial challenges that would certainly come with it. But when I forged ahead and established a nonprofit sanctuary for great apes, she was encouraging and supportive. The Center for Great Apes provides a home for over fifty chimpanzees and orangutans who formerly either were in entertainment or were private pets.

Years later, Jane visited me and the rest of the people involved in this project at our rural Florida location. After meeting all our chimps, including Michael Jackson's one-time pet, Bubbles, and a special-needs juvenile with cerebral palsy, Knuckles, Jane spent most of her time visiting with Grub and grooming him. Grub had a special fondness and talent for tearing holes in scraps of paper, making "masks," and then giving them to visitors. He made a lovely mask for Jane and pushed it through the mesh for her. She immediately wore the mask that Grub made and then pant-hooted to him, which pleased Grub immensely.

When Grub died unexpectedly at the age of twenty from cancer, the grief I felt was immobilizing. Since he had been the first chimpanzee I ever cared for, Grub was very special. The bond was strong, and I was devastated. Jane wrote me a letter that helped me get back on track: "Indeed, I know the deep sadness of losing special chimpanzee friends. Grub will be remembered by many. He is enshrined in your heart and mind. The more you love, the more you grieve. But there are all those others who also matter so, so much." I have long cherished that letter and those words.

PATTI RAGAN is the founder and director of the Center for Great Apes, which has rescued more than fifty orangutans and chimpanzees from the entertainment industry, research laboratories, and the exotic pet trade. For over twenty years, this sanctuary in Wauchula, Florida, has cared for these apes.

A Soft-Spoken Woman

LESLIE DAY

Dr. Jane is a soft-spoken woman with a loud voice for those who cannot speak for themselves. Her ability to positively influence those who do not share her opinion has always amazed me.

I have always been in awe of Dr. Jane and was very excited to share our sanctuary with her when she first arrived in 2005. During that visit, after all her official duties were complete, Dr. Jane took the time to sit down with caregivers and volunteers at her feet, tell stories, answer questions about her experiences, and share her dreams for a better world. Both of Dr. Jane's visits to our community have made a huge impact and left us with hope for a better tomorrow.

LESLIE DAY is the founder and president of Oregon's only chimpanzee sanctuary, Chimps Inc., created in 1995 to care for adult chimpanzees discarded from the pet and entertainment industries.

A Chimp in Need Has a Friend Indeed in Dr. Jane

IAN REDMOND

In 1989, I discovered firsthand how Jane Goodall can make things happen.

On behalf of the International Primate Protection League (funded by the late Cyril Rosen), I was investigating the commercial bushmeat trade in Congo-Brazzaville and the resulting flood of gorilla and chimp orphans. Commercial poachers were shooting adult apes for meat and selling any surviving orphaned babies as pets. (Both of these activities are illegal.)

I had just returned from my first visit there and was in Pointe Noire, a busy port on the Atlantic coast and Congo's second city. In the so-called Parc Zoologique, I photographed the rows of stark barren cages, their presence a testimony to the former flow of animals through that port during the French colonial period. Far from being a zoological park, the Pointe Noire "zoo" may have originally been a collection of holding cages designed for the temporary storage of animals before shipment to France. After Congo became an independent nation in 1960, the place was given its grand title of Parc Zoologique, but the facilities and care were anything but grand. Rather than being actively acquired, most of the residents were orphaned babies or abandoned pets.

There were nine chimpanzees, two mandrills, and a moustached monkey—some of them barely alive. Although it is likely that gorillas arrived there periodically (it being the only place in town with reasonably secure cages), I saw none. However, baby chimps are much hardier than baby gorillas and so survive for longer. That would explain why there were nine chimps and no gorillas.

Seldom had I experienced a more depressing ordeal than that visit to the Pointe Noire "zoo." There was no entrance gate. We just drove around the back of a row of houses into what looked like a large, neglected garden with a series of brick single-story buildings with corrugated-iron roofs. Each building had a row of open-fronted cells with thick wire mesh to keep in the animals. Many of the cages were empty or being used as storage cupboards, but the few that contained animals were truly shocking. The concrete floors and walls were caked with dried feces, and in the gloomy interiors, skeletal primates stared out dully with vacant eyes. Without exaggeration, it resembled nothing less than a chimpanzee concentration camp.

My colleagues and I gave the animals what food and water we had but could do little more on the spot. We were told that a well-wisher had given some money to refurbish the cages, but it had been spent on new roofing. The result was that even when it was pouring with rain, the water flowed off the roof, out of reach of the animals, who were clearly suffering in the heat. I offered my bottle of water to thirsty lips protruding through the mesh and began to pour. What surprised me was the behavior of the other chimps—watching intently but not pushing or fighting for access. This was serious. They patiently waited their turn, apparently not wanting to spill a drop, as I moved from one to another pouring pure cold water into parched mouths. The memory lives with me to this day.

When I returned to England, I could not find a major newspaper willing to run an article with these photos to kick-start a campaign that might do something about the ape trade. I did, however, show them to Jane at her home in Bournemouth, England. She was greatly moved by the images and immediately arranged for a volunteer to travel to Brazzaville. Within days someone was there to improve the diet and care of those suffering primates. Soon after, Alliette Jamart, a compassionate Pointe Noire resident who was moved by their plight, set up HELP-Congo and successfully rehabilitated these particular chimpanzees into a natural habitat in an area called Conkouati—now a national park. And to begin to deal with the continuing flow of babies from the bushmeat trade, the Jane Goodall Institute set up the Tchimpounga Chimpanzee Rehabilitation Center not far from Pointe Noire.

Meanwhile, in Brazzaville, the capital of Congo-Brazzaville, the city zoo also had a collection of primates, including the amazingly long-lived but skeletal chimpanzee known as Gregoire, who endured conditions not that much better than those in Pointe Noire. Thanks to Jane, Gregoire's enclosure and care were improved, and he was eventually moved to Tchimpounga to live out his days in relative comfort. He died there in 2008 at the age of sixty-six, Africa's oldest-known chimpanzee and a national hero. Over time, Tchimpounga grew to house more than 150 chimps and became Africa's largest ape sanctuary, the existence of which enables the Congo authorities to confiscate illegally held chimpanzees.

While Jane Goodall is just one person, she inspires and enables many others to do more. Now, as one of the most dynamic octogenarians on the planet, Dr. Jane continues to make things happen and inspires others to improve the lives of all chimpanzees, indeed all animals, including humans, all over the world.

IAN REDMOND is a wildlife biologist and conservationist known for his work with great apes and underground elephants. A self-confessed gorilla-holic since 1976, he chairs the Ape Alliance. Some of his best friends have been gorillas.

Gombe: A Virology Laboratory

BEATRICE H. HAHN

I was surprised and, yes, excited when we heard that Dr. Jane Goodall would allow us to test fecal and urine samples from Gombe chimpanzees for the chimpanzee counterpart of Human Immunodeficiency Virus type I (HIV-1), which we refer to as the Simian Immunodeficiency Virus, type chimpanzee (SIVcpz). As we soon discovered, the chimpanzees at Gombe were naturally infected with SIVcpz. We also showed that we could use their droppings to diagnose and molecularly characterize this virus in chimps, who were habituated to human observers enough that the identities of individuals were well established.

Having the Gombe virus sample was hugely important because it allowed us to rigorously test our methods by analyzing samples from known individuals under code. By documenting the presence of SIVcpz-specific antibodies in urine and fecal samples, and by amplifying viral sequences from fecal RNA, we were able to validate our noninvasive approach. This, in turn, allowed us to study other nonhabituated ape populations and ultimately to trace the origin of the human AIDS virus

(HIV-1) to a geographically isolated chimp population in southeastern Cameroon. To be sure, the presence of SIVcpz among the Gombe chimps was also bad news, particularly since it turned out that this infection was, in fact, pathogenic, causing immunodeficiency and a chimp version of AIDS in infected individuals.

Looking toward the future, it is my sincere hope that by Jane's ninetieth birthday, we will have a road map to combat SIVcpz infections at Gombe without interfering in the lives of the chimpanzees. Using novel intervention strategies that have been developed for HIV-1 infected humans, we hope eventually to drive SIVcpz in Gombe to extinction. This would be the ultimate *thank-you* to both Jane and her chimpanzees.

BEATRICE H. HAHN, professor of medicine at the University of Pennsylvania, is known for developing noninvasive methods to study microbes infecting endangered primate species in the wild.

Jane the Ambassador

IRENE PEPPERBERG

I was in high school in the 1960s, when women were still expected not to work outside the home, except maybe before marriage or possibly later as an elementary school teacher. Although I loved animals, I didn't expect to have a career in animal behavior. I was fascinated by chemistry, in fact, and was desperately looking for a role model of a woman scientist who had a career doing exactly what she wanted.

Stories of a researcher living among the apes in Africa—Jane Goodall—

provided me with a living example of a woman who had a mind of her own and lived an extraordinary life. When my high school guidance advisor tried to get me to apply to an all-women's college that would not foster a serious interest in science, I thought of Jane and rebelled. I ended up at MIT. When it came time for graduate school, the feminist movement was still several years in the future, and although no one discouraged me from applying to places like Harvard and Yale, I had to justify why a slot should go to someone likely to, as it was said, "get married, get pregnant, and leave the field, wasting the expense of her education." Again, I thought of Jane and forged ahead.

After switching fields, I would meet Jane briefly at various symposiums, but it was only many years later, when asked to introduce her at a fundraising event in Tucson, that I really came to appreciate her dedication to conservation and to the animals and land she works to conserve. She showed everyone in that room that it was not enough to be a scientist and present data, amazing as that might be, but that one also had to be a passionate, active, and engaging ambassador: to be the spokesperson on behalf of those who could not present their case to the world.

Recently, I learned that Jane has expanded her conservation efforts to a creature closest to my heart, the African Grey Parrot. The currently serious problem of parrot poaching is likely to become of even greater importance in the near future. Although many rules and regulations exist that supposedly prohibit or limit importing Greys into the United States and almost all Grey parrots now sold as pets come from reputable breeders, the breeding population is becoming elderly, and most domestically bred parrots do not make good breeders. Thus, rumors have emerged suggesting that a few people in the business of breeding Greys are talking about the need to import "new blood." This horrific possibility needs to be stopped in its tracks, and having Jane Goodall as the Grey Parrots' defender will make a huge difference in the lives of these birds and all creatures who share their world.

IRENE PEPPERBERG is a parrot-language researcher in the psychology department at Harvard University.

Bear Ambassador Jane

JILL ROBINSON

I think of Jane every time I clean my teeth.

Several years ago, the words in one of her presentations to spellbound students in China resonated with me—when I heard her talking about the millions of gallons of precious water wasted across the world when people leave the tap running as they brush their pearly whites. I was guilty as charged, and I never left the tap running again.

I think of Jane with love and gratitude for her legacy of compassion, remembering one of her visits to our bear sanctuary in China and the day she helped us in a health check. She saw a bear arriving from one of the country's cruel and notorious "farms," shed tears for the wounded shell of an animal who had been caged and mutilated, and spoke so kindly and memorably to a team trying to help him. She saw him being cut out of his crude cage, helped to clip his claws—and named him Mandela, in recognition of his forgiveness after being imprisoned behind bars for so many years. At the end of the health check she gently kissed this sleeping bear on his nose, and then reached over to kiss mine. I think of Jane when I walk past our Bear House 6 and see Mandela playing with his friends today in giddy somersaults of play. This handsome, peaceful bear, who suffered incomprehensible agony in his past, is today a ridiculously happy soul who charms staff and visitors alike with his love and enjoyment of simply being a bear.

Today, Jane continues helping the bears and will speak out for them and against bear-bile farming wherever she finds young aspiring biologists, zoologists, and welfarists wondering just exactly what they can do. Thus, I think of Jane when her teaching comes full circle, and I see children visiting us and gushing about all the projects they're carrying out in the name of Roots & Shoots. I recognize their pride and excitement of growing up as little ambassadors, breaking through the brick walls of the world's problems and feeling a satisfaction at what their work is doing.

Adored by millions the world over, this Messenger of Peace and all-round workaholic who never stays in one place for more than three weeks at a time has inspired a revolution of change that can start from such absurdly simple steps . . . including the one of turning off the tap while brushing one's teeth.

JILL ROBINSON has been a pioneer of animal welfare in Asia. In 1998 she founded Animals Asia, an organization devoted to ending the barbaric practice of bear-bile farming and to improving the welfare of animals in China and Vietnam.

Of Knitting, Birds, and Jane

CARA BLESSLEY LOWE

Understand one thing. I never set out to save animals.

Nebraska, the Platte River, 2002: I was knitting a scarf, and as it was my first, it was a time-consuming proposition.

I can see her now—Jane at a rolltop desk. Next to her, a telephone of the sort you don't see any more, the kind with the little holes in a rotating dial. Dusk. The cranes are kerr-looing behind her, and somewhere back there, in the thicket of riparian tangle, a raccoon ambles, pillaging another birdfeeder under the cover of pending night.

It is her first visit to the Platte, and she has fallen in love with its springtime: the bare promise of cottonwoods not yet leafed out, and most of all, masses upon masses of sandhill cranes. Each cry adds to a chorus of avian cacophony that here, now, somehow fuses into a single symphony of wildness.

The words are not quite an admonition, and they fall just shy of a warning. "You'll not finish that scarf, you know. Saving animals won't allow time for that."

The sun drops. The birds settle. A fire is built. Scotch is poured. An annual tradition is born. Years pass. Eventually a decade.

The scarf, as forecast, goes unfinished.

CARA BLESSLEY LOWE is an author, documentary filmmaker, and cofounder of the Cougar Fund, a nonprofit devoted to protecting cougars and their fellow animals.

Wild Camel Meets Chimp Champion

JOHN HARE

Wild camel and chimpanzee: that odd relationship was cemented in 1997 when Dr. Jane Goodall consented to become the life patron of the Wild Camel Protection Foundation. This is the only foundation in the world solely committed to save from extinction critically endangered wild double-humped camels in their pristine habitat in the Gobi deserts of China and Mongolia.

I rang Jane up, initially, based on the most tenuous of connections. My wife's aunt had worked in an office with Jane's mother before World War II, and they had become good friends. But Jane's generosity and willingness to embrace so much meant that after our very first meeting she gave her consent. Since then, we have not only become firm friends, but Jane has helped the critically endangered wild camels to survive and increase in number.

Her help has taken many forms, but mainly it has been through putting me (and the wild camels) in touch with her contacts and connections all over the world. She has also written most generously about our foundation's efforts to establish a nature reserve in China and to set up a wild camel breeding center in Mongolia, the only place in the world where the wild camel is held in captivity.

I don't think Jane had heard of wild camels when we first met or knew that they were the eighth-most critically endangered large mammals in the world. She was impressed by their tenacity to cling to life in the harshest of deserts—the Gobi—and indeed to have survived forty-three atmospheric nuclear tests when their prime habitat became China's premier nuclear test site. At the same time, these remarkable creatures stayed alive on saltwater slush with a higher content of salt than seawater, not because they preferred salt water, but because their worst enemy—humans—had forced them to the edge of existence.

Jane's passion for her numerous causes, her life-changing books, her serene character—a person at peace with herself—combine to put her into my personal locker of unforgettable personalities. When wild camels were identified as a totally new and separate species in 2008, Jane was one of the first to offer her congratulations. But it is to her that congratulations are due.

JOHN HARE founded the Wild Camel Protection Foundation, which is dedicated to protecting from extinction the wild double-humped camel.

Lessons from Jane

GAIL HUDSON

I first met Jane in 2005 in someone's home in Seattle. A mutual friend had asked me to help her finish *Harvest for Hope: A Guide to Mindful Eating*. Jane didn't know me then. I only knew the public image of Jane Goodall. But I brought her a bouquet of a dozen pastel pink roses, hoping this offering would help bridge the unknown distance between us.

I wasn't sure if the roses worked, but I saw that she appreciated my push-up-your-sleeves-and-get-to-work mind-set, even as she smiled bemusedly at my seriousness sometimes. After that initial meeting, we agreed to embark on our first writing journey together. I happened to know the landscape well—that of sustainable agriculture. Hurriedly and determinedly we crafted Jane's manifesto for mindful eating.

Once that journey was complete, Jane invited me on other adventures in writing, and we began to explore worlds that were more familiar to her but more foreign to me. In *Hope for Animals and Their World* she introduced me to people who were helping to save endangered species from extinction. And most recently, in *Seeds of Hope*, she led me into the rich and lush world of the plant kingdom.

Seeing the world through the eyes of a compassionate naturalist has inspired me to be more attuned to the life around me. Dare I say she has expanded my sense of the sacred? I speak with trees now. I touch leaves and study their veins. I listen for what the plants have to say. I look into animals' eyes and feel more responsibility and urgency to use the written word as my sword and do what I can to protect them. I am more apt to seek the goodness in humanity and have faith in our potential to make things right. This part of Jane—the nontraditional scientist, who refuses to separate the mind from the heart, who refuses to abandon hope in the face of our tumultuous world—has strengthened me.

Which brings me back to the roses. Many years after we met, she told me that roses are one of her favorite flowers. Yes! I felt a kind of prideful moment, having trusted my intuition and chosen the right offering for out first meeting. But there is something more about the rose that I wish to say.

While working on *Seeds of Hope*, Jane shared a story about a rose that was created and named in her honor. The Jane Goodall rose is soft pink, like the inside of a shell, and when it fully blooms, a golden-orange glow illuminates the center. This rose has delighted her thoroughly. I like to think of this rose as embodying the strengths of Jane, the gentle pink of her tender, compassionate heart holding the burning orange of her brilliant intelligence. This marriage of heart and mind—and how it creates a force far greater than the sum of its parts—is what she has mentored for me. Perhaps this is one of the most powerful teachings I've ever learned.

Oh, but there are a few more things I've learned from Dame Jane Goodall—an appreciation of fine scotch and the need for laughter and lightness even as we look face-on into the darkness. For all of these gifts, along with her gift of friendship, I am forever grateful.

GAIL HUDSON, a Seattle-based writer, editor, and life coach, has collaborated on three books with Jane Goodall, most recently *Seeds of Hope: Wisdom and Wonder from the World of Plants*.

My Dr. Jane Saga

VIVIAN B. WHEELER

In the 1980s, when I was senior manuscript editor in the sciences at Harvard University Press (HUP), I was assigned to work with an author new to us—Dr. Jane Goodall. We were to publish her magnum opus, a summary of the important research she had compiled over the previous twenty-some years. I met Jane briefly when she came to Cambridge to sign on; then she vanished into the wilds of Africa. As I set to work, combing through piles of blue tissue paper—some typed, some handwritten—many questions arose. Communication with Africa being what it was in those days, HUP's director decided to send me out to consult with Dr. Jane in person.

It would be a trip I'll never forget. After a long-thwarted telephone conversation with Dr. Jane, I began collecting what she'd requested—prescriptions, salves, baby items (whether for herself, her observers, her dogs, or her chimps I wasn't always sure), and a particular kind of cheese. The owner of the local cheese shop insisted on *giving* me the variety of cheese that Jane had requested. She was a real fan, and so I had the right kind of cheese. We had arranged to meet in Switzerland, so at least I wouldn't have to go off to Africa all by myself. During my overnight stop there, however, the "Blizzard of the Century" hit, and the famed Swiss precision blew apart. Nothing moved. At last, one small plane was departing for

Africa, but Jane was not at the airport! All my possessions and the manuscript were already on board, so I departed alone for a continent on which
I knew no one. A scary middle-of-the-night stop in Jeddah brought armed
soldiers on board, but eventually I arrived in Dar.

Two days later an exhausted Jane showed up, and I gave her the things
I had brought, including the special cheese. When she heard about the
cheese lady, Jane had me take a picture of her cutting into some of the
cheese on a large tray. She then autographed the photo, which I eventually returned to the incredibly grateful cheese lady back home.

Back with Jane in Dar es Salaam our friendship grew, and lots of sat-
isfying work was done. Then she invited me to accompany her to Gombe
for one of her periodic observation tours. Since Dr. Jane was bumped from
her flight, we rode instead for two or three days cross-country on a pretty
basic Tanzanian train.

Once in Kigoma, we pulled out the boat kept for Jane's excursions. A
simple Zodiac, it did get us the hundred miles up Lake Tanganyika to
Gombe—and the chimpanzees. I treasure my photo of a wind-blown Dr.
Jane at the helm. Amid glorious scenery, we arrived at Jane's hut on the
beach, only to realize that it was locked. While one of the locals ran five
miles to fetch the key, Jane darted off to see the chimps. That left me
alone to deal with the baboons greedily eyeing our provisions. Easy—I
had a broom!

When we walked "upstairs" the next morning, I had the special joy
of seeing chimpanzees firsthand. Getty, then an adorable infant, was
my favorite. I didn't care much for Goblin, who was in alpha mode and
charged me. Early on, Jane taught me a valuable lesson: this territory
belonged to the animals, not the humans, and so we gave way to them.
She and I fell into a routine whereby I worked on the manuscript, she

followed chimps, and in the evening we reviewed the editorial changes, enjoyed a swim in the lake, and devoured a stew supper with three M&Ms for dessert.

Many more experiences, and too soon, it was a week later—time for us both to leave. Back in the boat, we discovered the engine wouldn't start, and we drifted farther and farther from shore. Fortunately, one of the men saw our plight and swam out to get us going. We then whizzed back to Kigoma at top speed and then, once again in Dar, we were feted by some of her wonderful friends. Before I knew it, I was on a flight back to Boston.

In 1986 *The Chimpanzees of Gombe* was published to wide critical acclaim and countless awards. I cherish the letters I received from both the author and her mother, Vanne. Jane's "big book" has inspired readers the world over. As I live today next to the ocean, care for my own rescue cat, and volunteer at the local animal shelter, I know that these efforts stem from my time with Dr. Jane and the chimpanzees. My outlook on animals has been forever altered. The cheese lady, M&Ms, Skipper Jane, the care packages given to us by friends—these have special meaning to me and undoubtedly to Jane as well. Many, many friends have heard my Dr. Jane story, including my grandchildren's scout troops. I am honored to know Jane. I can never thank her enough for the inspiration she has given me and for remaining my true friend over all these years.

Blessings on you, dear one, and may you continue your wondrous work for *many* years to come!

During the twenty years VIVIAN B. WHEELER spent as manuscript editor at Harvard University Press, she edited several hundred books, mostly in the sciences. The most memorable, for many reasons, was Jane Goodall's *Chimpanzees of Gombe*.

Thank You, Jane

CHARLES KNOWLES

Like many American children of the 1960s, I grew up watching Jane in the forests of Gombe as portrayed by *National Geographic*. I always dreamed that I could be her, but alas, my path has been a far different one.

After completing my graduate degree at Stanford in computer science and business, I went to work in Silicon Valley. I had the good fortune to retire by the time I was thirty-five, and then I was left with the question, What do I do now? I returned to my childhood passion for wildlife conservation and began helping Laurie Marker grow the Cheetah Conservation Fund (CCF) in Namibia. Mostly this took the form of organizing fundraisers and helping to expand the reach of CCF in the United States.

Several years later a local reporter contacted me and said, "Charlie, you're famous!" to which I replied, "Excuse me?" He responded, "I was just interviewing Jane Goodall, and she said that what she really needed was a Charlie Knowles." I had never met Jane, and naturally I was deeply flattered, but mostly I was curious about how she could possibly need me.

I contacted JGI and invited Jane to visit me in Silicon Valley, where I hosted a small reception of supporters. One person I invited, Akiko Yamazaki, whom I had never met, responded to my invitation with, "I heard Jane speak in Kyoto and would love to come, but I'll be out of town. My husband and I have a small foundation, and I would love to meet with you to talk about conservation." It turned out that Akiko's husband is Jerry Yang, the founder of Yahoo.

Over lunch Akiko and I talked about wildlife conservation and decided to create the Wildlife Conservation Network (WCN). Jane was kind enough to speak at our second conference and has returned an additional five times. Never once has she asked for a speaker's fee, and she has always been immensely generous with her time. There is no question that her presence, her passion, and her endorsement of the WCN model is directly responsible for what WCN is today: a world-class organization that has raised and deployed over $35 million funding wildlife conservation in thirty countries.

Thank you, Jane. You touched my life when I was a little boy, and you continue to have a huge impact on me today. You not only inspired me and were the catalyst for me starting WCN, but you've also continued to be the spark that rallies people to the cause of saving wild animals and wild places.

CHARLES KNOWLES founded the software company Rubicon Technology in 1989 and sold it in 1994. His retirement lasted six days. In 2002 he cofounded the Wildlife Conservation Network to identify and invest in the world's best and brightest conservationists.

Proud to Call Her a Partner

WAYNE PACELLE

Looking back to my own childhood, I can see that the right set of influences somehow made compassion for animals a dominant emotional impulse in my life. Jane Goodall was one of my mentors. I was one of the millions of readers of *National Geographic* who were her wide-eyed students. She took us on field trips that were otherwise beyond our reach. With some help from the magazine, she shrank the world and introduced us to other cultures, both human and nonhuman.

I was fascinated by animals even then, and I anxiously awaited
the arrival of each month's issue. When it finally came, I immediately
scanned its contents to find the profile of the wild animal species gracing
each issue. I'd get especially excited when it was about wolves or chimps,
and, of course, Jane was the one who translated chimp behavior and gave
us special insights into their cultures. She reminded us all that animals
are not just machines, operating on instinct. They think and feel in ways
similar to how we think and feel.

I drew so much inspiration from Jane and her own courageous stands
for animals. In so many ways, she put an entirely nonthreatening face on
animal protection. Given her iconic status, who could disagree with this
woman? At a time when animal protection issues had become so polar-
ized, she transcended that divide and recruited countless people into our
ranks. Her speaking, her writing, and her gentle yet determined and resolute manner have made an extraordinary difference.

A few years ago, we at the Humane Society of the United States asked
an undercover investigator to apply for a job at the biggest chimpanzee
laboratory in the United States. She bravely documented the fear, the
isolation, and the pain endured by the creatures unlucky enough to be
caged in these facilities. When we released the footage, Jane validated our
work. She also demanded, standing right by our side, that the federal government get out of the business of warehousing chimps and conducting
invasive experiments on them. She asked that they be sent to sanctuaries.
It's taken many years of work, but together, working side by side, we've
achieved that result. Jane was always there to make a call to the director of the U.S. Fish and Wildlife Service, to the director of the National
Institutes of Health, or to a key elected official. Every one of those calls
made a difference. She's a uniquely powerful force in our movement.

I am a fan of Jane Goodall. But more than anything, I am an admirer. She did pioneering work on animal behavior and animal consciousness, and now she's doing pioneering work on human consciousness. We are all in her debt, and I am proud to call her a partner in this great cause of helping animals, curbing human-caused cruelty, and leaving places for animals to live in peace and safety.

WAYNE PACELLE is president and CEO of the Humane Society of the United States and the author of the *New York Times* best seller *The Bond: Our Kinship with Animals, Our Call to Defend Them*. He serves on the board of directors of several organizations.

JANE AS PROFESSOR

Between 1970 and 1975, Jane was a visiting professor who lectured on human biology at Stanford University in California. Human Biology was a new, cross-disciplinary major for undergraduates that offered traditional biology courses while also providing courses that focused more on what it means to be human. Considering humans as apes within the primate order was one way to do that, and Jane was brought in to talk about the apes she knew well, Gombe's wild chimpanzees. Stanford also maintained a small group of captive chimps who, released from captivity elsewhere in the United States, lived in a six-acre enclosure off campus where they could be studied under semi-natural conditions. But by far the most exciting part of the Human Biology major was the chance students were given to apply for a six-month stay in Gombe, doing real field research on chimps and baboons under the guidance of one of the world's legendary pioneers in primate studies.

The two essays opening this section, written by former Stanford undergraduates Emily Polis Gibson and Jim Moore, recall dealing with Jane in her professorial context at Stanford. Moore's essay goes further to touch on his experience at Gombe and some of the lessons Professor Jane taught there.

Most of the Stanford undergraduates did not intend to spend their careers attending to the lives and welfare of nonhuman primates. Many of them, including John Crocker, instead entered careers that brought them to attend to the lives and welfare of the human primate. They became physicians, in other words, and yet their time spent in the forest among creatures who were not quite human marked the way they came to think of their later charges.

Annie Vander Stoep, who went on to become a teacher and researcher in child psychiatric epidemiology, describes the experience of being at Gombe as life-changing and her friendship with her former professor there lifelong.

There were also less positive, more bitter lessons to learn, including the truth that Gombe always contained hidden dangers, the lurking, ever-present risks of chaos and death—as became manifest in the 1975 kidnapping of four undergraduates. The students were eventually ransomed and released, but Stanford ended the Human Biology program. Phyllis C. Lee, who was a member of that disrupted last class and went on to become a field biologist herself, adds the observation that Jane's legacy from the Stanford years continues still, passed on to new generations of scientists, teachers, and students.

No doubt Jane was an exceptional professor in the classroom at Stanford. She was an even more exceptional one back at the university of the forest. Starting as early as the 1960s, in fact, advanced-degree students began coming out to learn from Jane and the animals. Many of these students were British and arrived through the arrangements of Jane's own former teacher and advisor at Cambridge University in England, Professor Robert Hinde. Four of Hinde's advisees—David Bygott, Jeannette Hanby, Richard Wrangham, and Anne Pusey—have contributed essays for this volume.

Robert Hinde was a major proponent and practitioner of ethology, the science of animal behavior. Jane was his star student, and Hinde sent her more students who were destined to shine. Coming to Gombe, they found "a window into the chimps' lives" (as Bygott writes) that was the result of Jane's "years of patient observation and habituation," so that the animals being watched tolerated the presence of the watchers. Jeanette Hanby was actually headed to the Serengeti to study lions, but she became romantically attached to Bygott, having met him through their shared association with Hinde. Thus she, too, came under Professor Jane's spell. Intrigued by the dynamics of social coherence among nonhumans, she found Jane's way of promoting her own group's coherence—the communal chimpanzee hoot—an interesting human adaptation. "Jane's a hooter," Hanby concludes, and also "a great ape." After doing his graduate work studying the Gombe chimpanzees, Richard Wrangham established a chimpanzee research site in Uganda's Kibale National Park. In his essay, Wrangham recalls the exciting early years at Gombe, describes a special lesson Jane taught him, and explains how that lesson came to inform his later research. Another of Hinde's advisees who became one of Jane's students, Anne Pusey, recalls the "burgeoning group of students" there and their wonderful sense of shared purpose. Pusey went on to rescue the rat- and rot-threatened records from many years of chimpanzee research by taking them to a more protected environment at the University of Minnesota (and later Duke University), where she began the Herculean task of organizing and transforming them into more permanent form.

Bygott, Hanby, Wrangham, and Pusey: to that gang of four, I add a fifth. Elizabeth Vinson Lonsdorf was an advisee of Anne Pusey before she came to Gombe. By the time Lonsdorf arrived, Jane had retired from research and begun her second career as an activist. Nonetheless, she periodically returned to the place where it all began. Lonsdorf recalls, during one of those special visits, being taught "how truly precious those moments are when you get to relax, talk, laugh, and share a drink with good friends."

Two other postdoctoral researchers, William C. McGrew and Linda F. Marchant, came from beyond the Stanford and Cambridge circuits to do research at Gombe. McGrew originally went there in 1972, interested in infant development and then tool use, and was impressed by Jane's listening skills as well as her ability to be an "Opener of Doors." In 1992, as a professor of anthropology at Miami University, he returned in the company of Linda

Marchant (also an anthropologist at Miami), who was interested in hand preference among the chimps. Her essay describes a teaching moment at the university of the forest when Professor Jane effectively passed on good advice
about how best to deal with an intellectual issue as well as a physical one.

I add to this section a few accounts by people who have been influenced by
Professor Jane during what might be called *teaching moments*. This provides
an image of Jane on the move, Jane as the peripatetic professor. Those who
have come in contact with this Jane discover that she is a master teacher who
combines an expert's deep knowledge of a subject with the capacity to listen
and, in listening, to understand what is missing, needed, or not yet grasped.
Carol Gigliotti, a teacher herself, describes that aspect of the peripatetic professor's style: listening with full attention. Joe Duff, whooping crane conservationist, beautifully describes a teaching moment during which, in a simple
yet inspired fashion, Jane taught him to see that "there is poetry in flying with
cranes." Virginia Morell, author of a biography of the Leakey family, recalls a
teaching moment that occured at Gombe. Shadrack Mkolle Kamenya, director
of conservation for the Jane Goodall Institute in Tanzania, provides a fresh
vision of Jane as someone who teaches by example. The details Kamenya
shares are, I think, telling: her respectful style of walking through the forest,
the care she takes in avoiding waste, the respect she shows to others. She is
a "unique naturalist," and what she has to teach cannot be taught in a school,
for "there is no school to train us to be like her." And, finally, as Jane's long-
time friend and collaborator, I recall some of my own experiences with "Jane
the Teacher."

The section ends with essays by Gloria Grow and Hamid R. Hossaini, both
students of the peripatetic professor at a remove: in her global, online university. Grow refers to one of Jane's television documentaries that provides

lessons in how to handle a dangerously unhappy ape. Hossaini recalls advice from Professor Jane's online birthday party that led him to revise his plans for dealing with the bees in his chimney.

—D. P.

Standing outside a Door

EMILY POLIS GIBSON

Standing outside a door in a long, dark, windowless hallway of offices at the Stanford Medical Center, I took a deep breath and swallowed several times to clear my dry throat. I hoped I had found the correct office, as there was only a number—no nameplate to confirm who was inside.

I was about to meet a childhood hero. I had read every one of her books and watched every TV documentary she'd ever made. I knocked with what I hoped was the right combination of assertiveness and humility. I heard a soft voice on the other side say, "Come in," so I slowly opened the door.

It was a bit like going through the wardrobe to enter Narnia. Bright sunlight streamed into the dark hallway as I stepped over the threshold. Squinting, I stepped inside and quickly shut the door behind me as I realized there were at least four birds flying about the room. They were taking off and landing, hopping about and feeding on birdseed on the office floor and the window sill. The windows were flung wide open with a spring breeze rustling papers on the desk. The birds looked very happy occupying the sparsely furnished room, which contained a desk, two chairs, a filing cabinet, and Dr. Jane Goodall.

She stood up and extended her hand, saying, "Hello, I'm Jane," and she offered me the other chair when I told her my name. She was slighter than she appeared when speaking at a lectern or on film. Sitting back down at her desk, she excused herself for a moment as she finished marking papers.

It was disorienting. In the middle of a bustling urban office complex containing nothing resembling plants or a natural environment, I had stepped into a bird sanctuary instead of sitting down for a job interview. I wasn't sure what I was supposed to do or say. Jane didn't look directly at me, yet I knew I was being observed. So I waited, watching the birds making themselves at home in her office, and slowly feeling at home myself. I felt my tight muscles start to relax, and I loosened my grip on the arms of the chair.

There was silence except for a twittering of finches as they flew about our heads. After a while she spoke, her eyes still perusing the papers before her: "It is the only way I can tolerate being here for any length of time. They keep me company. But don't tell anyone; the people here would think this is rather unsanitary."

I said the only thing I could think of: "I think it is magical. It reminds me of home."

Only then did she look at me. "Now, tell me why you'd like to come work at Gombe. . . ."

The next day I received a note from her letting me know I was accepted for the research assistantship. I had proven I could sit silently and expectantly, waiting for something, or perhaps nothing at all, to happen. For a farm girl who had never before traveled outside the United States, I was about to embark on an adventure far beyond the barnyard.

EMILY POLIS GIBSON is a wife, mother, farmer, writer, family physician, and director of student health services at Western Washington University in Bellingham.

What Jane Taught Me

JIM MOORE

My earliest memory is of finding a dead moray eel on a rope dangling from a pier near my home in Wailupe, Hawaiʻi. I grew up knowing absolutely that I would become a marine biologist, and as an undergrad at Stanford University I focused initially on marine invertebrate ecology, spending happy hours studying barnacles in Chuck Baxter's lab. But then something happened, and I became a primatologist.

I was taking Human Biology 2, and Jane Goodall was lecturing on animal behavior. A teacher excited by her subject is always fun, but when the apparently shy Dr. Goodall pant-hooted to the class, I started to pay real attention. Rather than the population/taxonomic perspective I'd always had, she was presenting animals as individuals with their own interests and histories, and it was fascinating. And then one day she showed us a draft of the film *Wild Dogs of Africa*. I walked straight from that exotic vision of research in Tanzania over to an organic chemistry midterm. Halfway through the test, I walked out, having decided to change majors and become a behaviorist. Two years later I went to Gombe as a research assistant.

While the course of my life was altered by Jane, most of my actual education about primates came from other directions once I got to graduate school. She did, though, teach me at least two important things.

First, the importance of the individual. This key insight of hers lies at the heart of modern behavioral ecology (the individual as evolved strategist), though Jane arrived at it orthogonally to, and ahead of, sociobiology. It is also at the core of more recent work on behavioral syndromes (aka personality) in animals, and it is hard to imagine what the field of animal behavior would look like today without that focus on individuals rather than populations or archetypes. Without Jane, the field would have arrived there anyway—since so many converging intellectual threads were heading that way—but not as quickly, and I would probably be studying intertidal invertebrates.

She also taught me to strive for integrity in my beliefs . . . and to respect snakes. I've always been fascinated by snakes, but I know some can be fatal. So it was mind-opening for me to talk with Jane about the boomslang who regularly passed in and out of her house and whom she regarded as another resident along with the geckos, spiders, and other critters we all lived with at Gombe, where most buildings were screened with 2" × 2" mesh that kept only large animals out. I mean, I was OK wih the green mamba passing through my hut periodically, but I didn't have a young child. She did. I realized that her acceptance of the small but real risk of a poisonous snakebite was a deep part of an overall ethic of living with . . . well, with everything. It had a profound effect on me in ways that I still discover today.

JIM MOORE has studied the behavioral ecology of modern primates using insights gained from such work to aid our understanding of Plio-Pleistocene hominids.

Looking Back

JOHN CROCKER

In July 2009, I returned to Gombe. It had been thirty-six years since I worked there with Jane on the mother-infant study of the chimps. Sitting at "the Peak" during that visit, I reflected on how Jane and the chimps influenced my style of medical practice, my parenting, and my worldview. Gazing down at the lush valleys below, I felt a profound appreciation for Jane and for the opportunity she provided me as a student to learn from her and the chimp mother-infant pairs Fifi and Freud, and Melissa and Gremlin.

As a family doctor and father, I have incorporated lessons I learned at Gombe about the crucial nurturing a young primate needs to be successful, especially a strong emotional bond, close physical contact, and reassurance from a parent. Jane modeled these behaviors with her son, Grub, and shared how a chimp mother's patience and gentle guidance enable her offspring to explore their surroundings with confidence and learn to survive in the wild. Now, when I witness my curious young patients rocketing around the exam room, I remember Jane's example and Fifi's patience with her son Freud's uninhibited and joyful behavior. And I constantly remind myself to be patient with my own two sons.

Jane also taught me to view human behavior from an evolutionary perspective. As a result, I developed a deeper understanding of aggression, depression, and anxiety. I see how our actions and reactions are hardwired for survival, and this has helped inform my decisions as a physician. I could see the similarities between the constant anxiety my adult patient Robert felt as he sat mired in traffic and the chimp Figan's building tension as he patrolled his community's border. Whereas Figan could release his pent-up energy through displays or grooming, though, we humans usually have to find other methods, such as practicing relaxation and getting regular exercise.

I am especially grateful to Jane for the sense of spirituality and confidence I gained at Gombe. In the book *Africa in My Blood*, Jane's editor

Dale Peterson notes, "As [Jane] came closer to nature and animals, she came closer to herself and in tune with the spiritual power she felt all around." As an uncertain young adult, I experienced a similar awakening through my interactions with Jane and my own quiet observations in the forest. Years later, Jane shared with me a ritual that beautifully reflects her nature-based spirituality. During a Seattle visit, as we chatted on a deck overlooking a cluster of trees in late afternoon, she gazed up at the sky at some puffy clouds and said, "I guess it's time for a toast to the Cloud Contingent." Since the deaths of close family and friends, Jane has referred to those precious people in her life as the Cloud Contingent, honoring their memory by connecting them with the constantly changing cloud formations.

JOHN CROCKER, happily married and with two sons, is a family doctor in Seattle, Washington.

Happy Birthday, Big Jane!
ANNIE VANDER STOEP

Dear Jane,

I am happy to have this chance to convey what indelible imprints you have left on my vocation, location, and family life. What a privilege it was to spend my junior year of college following Miff and Moeza and Melissa and Gremlin up and down the hills of Gombe, watching Wanda and newborn Wilke high in a tree as a special twenty-first birthday treat!

First, vocation. Observing young adolescent Flint lose the will to nourish himself or to socialize with his extended family and, finally, to live, as he grieved over the death of his mother, Flo, inspired me to conduct research to understand the factors contributing to poor emotional health in human children and to develop public health responses worldwide to the mental health conditions that compromise children's well-being.

Then, location. Your introduction to the magnificent inhabitants, human and non-, of the Serengeti Plains and the Gombe Stream lit in me a passion for East Africa. In recent years I have been able to teach mental health research methods to faculty and students at the University of Nairobi in Kenya. And this year, I fulfilled a dream of learning from face-to-face conversations and interviews with teachers, nurses, and parents in northern Malawi about the emotional health needs of their school-aged children.

Finally, family life. The planet is a better place with Big Jane and Little Jane on board! I can so clearly remember you holding four-month-old Jane on your lap and engaging her with soft pant-hoots. Raising your namesake has brought me unspeakable joy. Little Jane (turning thirty this month and 5 feet 7 inches tall) is strong, observant, inventive, independent, fun-loving, and full of life and the dickens. Her six-year-old daughter, Marley Mae, has a voracious appetite for natural history. Tomorrow I get to teach a social studies lesson on life in Kenya in her first-grade classroom. We'll wash our hands and eat *ugali*, sing the "Karibuni" song that I learned from the choir in Julius Nyerere's church, and look together at pictures of children dancing in northern Malawi.

ANNIE VANDER STOEP is a child psychiatric epidemiologist who teaches research methods and conducts etiologic and intervention research on child and adolescent mental health.

One of the Luckiest

PHYLLIS C. LEE

In the spring of 1975, I considered myself one of the luckiest undergraduates in the world. I was going to spend six months at Gombe Stream National Park studying primates under the supervision of Jane Goodall. I was probably one of the odder ones, as I was far more interested in the baboons than the chimpanzees—a difference of perspective I maintain to this day, probably much to Jane's dismay. The words *formative experience* do not do justice to that time at Gombe. Learning from Jane and the other amazing researchers at Gombe left me with a passion for observing animal behavior in detail and in the wild. The training was exceptional due to Robert Hinde, Jane's PhD supervisor at Cambridge, and his input into Gombe's excellent observational methods. Thanks to that unique Gombe experience, including learning about African birds from a real genius, I have retained my passion for science in nature.

It was unfortunately not a good time for Gombe, as this was the period of the violent hostage-taking by the anti-Mobutu gang of Joseph Kabila. With the kidnapping's resolution via the release of our friends, I ended up in south-central Tanzania in one of the most beautiful protected areas in the world. Jane put me to work habituating baboons and helping train the Tanzanian park rangers who were on baboon watch. Jane knew, even then, that science would only progress with comparative data from a number of field sites. And she supported me financially and logistically in Ruaha for six more months. My experiences in Ruaha combined with Jane's support at what was a catastrophic time for her, Gombe, and potentially the chimps, left me with an enduring passion for furthering our understanding and protection of African wildlife and their habitats. My thirty subsequent years of working with Cynthia Moss and the Amboseli elephants and close to forty years of research with primates across the globe began with those early, confused, and sometimes very anxious days at Gombe under Jane Goodall.

What is this legacy initiated by Jane? Since those Gombe-Ruaha days, I have been privileged to work with twelve PhD students who have studied both wild and captive chimpanzees, and another eighteen who have studied baboons, elephants, gorillas, colobus monkeys, macaques, capuchin monkeys, and muriquis, as well as humans and their ecosystems. I hope that this next generation of scientists, which has resulted directly from Jane Goodall and her encouragement of foundational studies on a variety of species at Gombe, will recognize and celebrate their intergenerational maternity.

PHYLLIS C. LEE is a professor of psychology at the University of Stirling. She was a Stanford University human biology major when she worked at Gombe in 1975.

You Changed My Life

DAVID BYGOTT

Dear Jane,

The year I graduated from university, 1969, I became fascinated by primate field studies. I pestered a number British primatologists, writing them to ask if they could use a research student. I was thrilled to hear back from the archbishop of animal behavior, Robert Hinde. There was a remote chance, he wrote, that I could find work as a research assistant for

Jane Goodall at Gombe! He then interviewed me, trying to scare me off with tales of incessant rain, hostile vegetation, steep and trackless terrain, isolation, malaria, and parasites that burrow under your toenails. "I'll go!" I insisted. He shrugged, and said that I'd better meet you.

So I came to your mother's flat in London. You received me graciously. I *had* to make a lasting impression and get this job.

"Would you like some tea or coffee?"

"Coffee, please. Black—er, with four sugars." That was not how I like it, but, in my desperation, I thought it might make me memorable.

"Ah, just like an African!" you said, laughing. "You'll fit in."

While I sipped my disgusting syrupy coffee, you briefed me on chimp work and camp life. Four-year-old Grub stood at the window, gazing beyond grayness to sunnier memories. A handsome, dark-haired man in a suit rushed through the room. "Hugo van Lawick," he explained. "Sorry, must run. See you later."

Our next encounter, some months later, was momentous for me. You invited me to join your family at Ngorongoro Crater until I could get to Gombe.

Ngorongoro? I had devoured Grzimek's book *Serengeti Shall Not Die*, and this was a dream come true. At a simple camp by the Munge River, you and Hugo were studying and photographing hyenas for your book *Innocent Killers*. For ten days, I shared that experience. By day, you typed your notes, and I sketched wildlife or helped Grub catch frogs in the muddy stream. We were surrounded by big game. Every evening, we piled into Land Rovers and followed the hyena pack. They were big and deadly. You could recognize each individual, and you recorded precise notes as they interacted. If a hunt began, the crash helmets went on, the coffee went out of the window, and Hugo set off in hot pursuit. I witnessed more amazing hyena behavior than I've ever seen since. A two-day foray to the heart of the Serengeti clinched it. I was hooked on the savannas.

But then came Gombe. For the next two years, I was part of a research team, young people who were daily watching chimps and other primates, and in that manner contributing to the long-term data pool or doing their own research. Although you seldom visited during those years, our precious window into the chimps' lives was solely due to your years of patient observation and habituation. I saw that wild chimps have a dignity and purpose and power that cannot be imagined by those who have only seen chimps in "jail." I came to know them intimately, to respect and care and even dream about them. Who could doubt that we were kin? I left part of my heart in Gombe and gained a new worldview—and some lasting human friends too, all of us bonded by that unique shared experience.

Back in Cambridge, England, and writing up my fieldwork, I met my life partner, Jeannette. Her boss—Robert Hinde—was my supervisor. And primate behavior (including our own) has kept us together for forty years.

After doing his doctoral research on the chimpanzees of Gombe, DAVID BYGOTT worked as a lion biologist in the Serengeti. He sketched gorillas for Dian Fossey and taught zoology at the University of Dar es Salaam. He guides safaris with Jeannette Hanby in East Africa.

Hoots

JEANNETTE HANBY

Can you hoot like a chimp? Like Jane? It's so uplifting! Imagine being surrounded by chimps in a forest, all hooting uproariously, excited, panting, puffing, and screaming. Then imagine being surrounded by humans in an audience, with Jane on the stage, starting a chimp hoot. I join, along with my mate and a few outliers, expressing the excitement that Jane can engender. Hooting together, howling together, marching together, working in a true team effort for chimps, for the planet. These are some of our joys living in a group. Jane is that rare human who can foster that feeling of collective *oneness*. That has been and still is her personal effect on me.

When I met Jane I didn't know how she would affect my life. I already knew of her, not only from films and books but also because my thesis advisor had been at Cambridge University with Jane when she earned her PhD. Her supervisor became mine, too. At Cambridge, I met one of Jane's research assistants, David Bygott, and married him. He'd been so smitten by Jane, the chimps, Gombe, and Tanzania that he was more than willing to return to Africa with me to study lions. On occasion, we overlapped with Jane, and I became increasingly aware of her ability to enlist that team spirit in her followers. I studied Jane's ways when I could. I watched how she got research organized and found funding for her projects. I remember a room full of shoes and powdered milk she'd got as donations for the chimp trackers. She did all this so earnestly, in difficult situations, and with her special wry humor.

When David and I camped out in Jane's home on the Tanzanian coast, the place was abuzz with mosquitos and rats in the toilets. I was impressed with Jane's survival skills in another dimension and her rapport with malaria, countless cups of tea, and great numbers of hangers-on. She coped with disappointments and distress, bureaucrats and paperwork, yet kept right on with research, writing, traveling, and lecturing. I knew I was different and couldn't juggle so many people and responsibilities at once. Even so, as one person in her little band of apes, I responded with increased determination on my own part to survive setbacks while working on conservation and education projects in Tanzania.

Jane was gracious about writing an introduction to our book on the lions we studied and lived with in the Serengeti. She is a master writer, and I've read most of her many contributions. That she thought our book and our work worth promoting bolstered my self-esteem. I've learned a lot from Jane, as well as from the chimps she and her band have studied for so long. Without her I wouldn't know the joy of a communal hoot, the team effort to preserve the animals and wild places we love. Jane's a hooter. She's a great ape—and you are, too, of course.

After earning a doctorate for her studies on Japanese monkeys, JEANNETTE HANBY came to Tanzania in 1974 to run the Serengeti Lion Project with David Bygott. For the last thirty years they have been guiding educational safaris in East Africa.

Be Open to Novel Observations

RICHARD WRANGHAM

Dear Jane,

In the summer of 1970, with little sense of my future other than wanting to be in the African wild, I wrote to you asking if you had any openings for research assistants. I was a newly minted graduate in zoology with no knowledge of primates, so my chances seemed low. But, amazingly, you summoned me to London. There I learned that you happened to be recruiting helpers. You even had money to cover them. A few weeks later you said yes. Not long after, I boarded a small plane in Nairobi taking some of your team to Kigoma, and my life changed forever.

I became part of a small group of students in Gombe. The atmosphere was heady. Advance notices of *In the Shadow of Man* were thrillingly positive. On your visits, you brought people with household names, and they reveled in your company. Big figures in science and culture had become part of your world. Still, in spite of the contact you gave us to that glitzy world, our and your deep excitement came from the life in the forest, not from that faint global buzz. Chimpanzees were this poorly understood bridge between humans and other animals, and Gombe was a bridge to them. It was a time of major discoveries. We who worked there began every day with the reasonable possibility of seeing a new clue that would expand humanity's understanding of chimpanzees. We were part of a revolution. I know that was how you felt too, so here is a little story about a dream coming true—a dream from my time in Gombe and long-ago discussions with you.

It happened this week at the research site I went on to establish in Kibale National Park, in western Uganda. Following two chimpanzees, young males both vying for the vacant alpha position, I took a video of them self-medicating with leaves. I could remember clearly when, in the early 1970s, you had said how wonderful it would be to have film footage of this extraordinary behavior: to document the careful picking and folding of individual hairy leaves (that happen to have a medicinal effect) and the swallowing of each, one by one. But chimpanzees do it so rarely, so briefly, and always in the gray light of dawn, that one has to be very lucky to catch that on film. Two days ago, it finally happened. The light was ideal, and Lanjo, our most habituated male, posed perfectly as he swallowed.

There was something else. The chimpanzees food-barked! They started giving those loud, passionate calls well before they reached the leaf-swallowing site, slid into a softer food-grunting after they arrived, and continued their vocal signals of contentment for a few minutes as they worked. One's first thought is that they were exceptionally excited about their strange "meal." But chimpanzees normally give food-calls only when eating the most delicious food, and it is hard to understand how hairy leaves that are swallowed could be experienced as even remotely delicious. The leaves have no obvious taste and, in any case, are not chewed at all. As you will remember from washing chimpanzee dung, one can find the leaves entire and undigested after they have traveled through the gut. Certainly the leaves' hairiness makes them horrid for humans (for me, at least!) to swallow. And once the few leaves are in the chimpanzee's otherwise empty stomach, it is also hard to imagine that they give any sense of fullness or digestive pleasure at all.

So what was going on? Why the excited food-barks? Was it a ploy? The two males seemed to be looking for others as they walked to the leaf site. They had been calling, listening, and smelling the ground where the paths forked. Maybe in their loneliness they had been trying to deceive others into joining them at the medicine patch. One of our former alpha males used to do something similar: he would give food-barks from a tree with no food. But there are other possibilities. Could they have been anticipating the good feelings that they were going to have a few hours later from the relief of stomach pain produced by the medicine they were swallowing? As you often say, with chimpanzees we see new things all the time.

I thought you would like this story of uncertainty because you were always encouraging your students to investigate anything new or puzzling. In long-ago Gombe, you spoke of a researcher in the Serengeti who, in the midst of dutifully collecting systematic data on his study species, noticed a bird of prey repeatedly flying up and dropping something from its talons. "What was the bird doing?" you had asked eagerly. "I don't know," came the researcher's reply. "I was in the middle of a focal observation. I didn't want to lose any data, so I couldn't stop to watch." You used to tell this story to show your research team what not to do. You wanted us to feel free to follow what was interesting. We were told to keep our eyes and minds open to whatever might reveal itself, even at the expense of a completed check sheet.

Your explicit encouragement to be open to novel observations helps explain the remarkable fact that the person whose career had taken a major step forward with observations of chimpanzee tool use was also the one who discovered tool use in Egyptian vultures. Even though you were not studying vultures, you noticed that they sometimes open ostrich eggs by throwing rocks at them. At first, the fact of your finding two fascinating but completely independent cases of animal ingenuity seemed odd. Had you been amazingly lucky, or were most other observers in the Serengeti strikingly shortsighted about recognizing what the Egyptian vultures were doing? Then I got to know you. Obviously it was not luck at all. It was attitude—one that was always open to anything unusual and then followed up with excitement and determination.

RICHARD WRANGHAM is the Ruth Moore Professor of Biological Anthropology at Harvard University and codirector of the Kibale Chimpanzee Project in western Uganda.

Gombe Chimpanzees Forever

ANNE PUSEY

My life changed when I found a London phone number in my college mailbox along with the instructions to call Jane Goodall. In my final year at Oxford, I had written to Professor Robert Hinde at Cambridge about graduate school, but I didn't know he had been Jane Goodall's advisor. As a matter of fact, I didn't even know who Jane Goodall was. But I dialed the number anyway.

My call was answered by Hugo van Lawick, Jane's husband, who said, "We study chimpanzees in Africa. We're looking for an assistant."

Wow! I had dreamed of studying animals in Africa, but in the male-dominated scientific world I saw around me, this had seemed impossible. I hastened to London for an interview. When I entered the room, I met Jane and Hugo along with their son, Grub. Then I was introduced to Jane's mother and Hugo's mother and brother. The entire family, it seemed, was gathered around and helping to choose photos for Jane and Hugo's book *Innocent Killers*. Incredible images of the Africa of my dreams were spread over the floor. My enthusiasm must have shone through my shyness, for by August 1970 I was on my way to Africa.

I found Jane sitting in her tent at Ndutu Lodge in the Serengeti, typing away at a draft of *In the Shadow of Man* as flocks of sand grouse swept past noisily. A week later we flew down to Kigoma in a small plane, then bumped across the waves of Lake Tanganyika in the local Baptist missionary's speedboat and arrived at Gombe at dusk. The next day, Jane led me to the feeding station, Grub on her arm, and there sat Flo and Flint. I was hooked.

For five years I followed mothers and infants, and then I studied the travails of adolescents as they left their mothers and integrated into the adult community. I was part of the burgeoning group of students Jane had gathered by then to study the chimpanzees and baboons. We lived and breathed their lives, gossiped about their exploits over dinner, talked with them in our dreams.

From my first days at Gombe, I was entranced by the filing cabinets of data. Details of the chimpanzees' behavior were documented daily in pages of dense typescript and color-coded charts. The pages were typed in quadruplicate, with copies sent to Cambridge and Nairobi. Thousands of photographs were stored. When Jane shifted her focus from research to activism in the late 1980s, I was very happy to be in a position to help her archive these data. We moved the dusty files—being ravaged by rodents on open shelves—to a safer home at the University of Minnesota and, later, Duke. Through the magic of computers, scanners, and the efforts of countless students, more than fifty years of data from twenty-six filing cabinets are now stored as digital images that fit on a hard drive hardly bigger than a cell phone. With births, deaths, and daily social interactions now in a database, we can trace, for example, the arc of Frodo's life from infancy through alpha male status to old age. We can also document this with photos and watch him on video. We can continue Jane's detective work of extracting patterns of behavior among our closest living relatives in order to understand better how they resemble and differ from ourselves.

And because of Jane's tireless fundraising, new generations of Tanzanian researchers and scientists from around the world are still following the descendants of chimpanzees she met and named in 1960, applying new scientific tools to extract DNA, hormones, and disease pathogens from feces in order to make discoveries that were simply unimaginable in 1960. How lucky I am to be part of this adventure and to have contributed to Jane's extraordinary study.

ANNE PUSEY is the J. B. Duke Professor of Evolutionary Anthropology at Duke University and director of the Jane Goodall Institute Research Center, which maintains the archive of long-term data on the Gombe chimpanzees.

Precious Moments

ELIZABETH VINSON LONSDORF

I remember clearly the first time I met Jane. I was an undergraduate at Duke University, and she came to speak at the thirtieth anniversary of the Duke Primate Center. I attended her talk with my mother, and afterward stood in line for a very long time waiting for her to autograph one of my *National Geographic* magazines, all the while trying to figure out what I would say to her. When it was finally my turn, I was dumbstruck. Nothing came out of my mouth. My mother laughs about it to this day as the only time she has ever seen me speechless.

A few years later I was in graduate school at the University of Minnesota working under the direction of Anne Pusey on the Gombe chimpanzee data. When I met Jane this time, I had finally found my voice, and so we had a very intense and exciting discussion about my various research ideas.

A couple of years after that, Jane and I were in Gombe walking in the forest together. To walk in the footsteps of my hero, or with my hero, in one of the most magical places on earth could have been a serious and overwhelming affair. But instead, it was relaxed and fun, with Jane at one point stopping to pick up and pretend to smooch a giant forest snail. Later that night in her house, over a glass of whiskey, she told hilarious and heartwarming stories about the early days at Gombe.

I felt lucky to be able to spend this time with her on a break from her incredibly rigorous schedule, to just relax and laugh for a while. I have now spent fifteen years studying the chimpanzees of Gombe, and almost everything I have learned about chimpanzees has its basis in Jane's work. But perhaps the most important thing she taught me is how truly precious those moments are when you get to relax, talk, laugh, and share a drink with good friends.

ELIZABETH VINSON LONSDORF is an assistant professor of psychology and biological foundations of behavior at Franklin and Marshall College. A researcher at Gombe since 1998, she has focused on chimp tool use, learning, health, and mother-infant interactions.

Opener of Doors

WILLIAM C. McGREW

Without Jane, I would never have met a chimpanzee. Sure, I'd have seen them in zoos, but to know them? Never. Jane gave me a chance. To be frank, I was not a likely prospect for Gombe, at least not by modern standards, having never studied nonhuman primates. But along with Caroline Tutin, who like me had recently received a PhD and was already funded to do research in another direction, I sought out Jane with more hope than confidence. She invited us to interviews in 1971 at Earl's Court in

London, and then she offered us places at Gombe. Presumably this was based on her intuition, as we had little else to offer.

Research clearance in Tanzania was hard to come by at that time, so after we'd cooled our heels for a few months, she arranged for us to meet some captive chimpanzees at the Delta Primate Center in Louisiana. There we had exclusive access for eight months to eight chimpanzees ranging in a 1.5-acre enclosure. It was a preview of things to come at Gombe, and the chimpanzees kept us busy recording their sexual behavior and tool use. During Jane's visit to Delta, the chimpanzees pulled off a mass escape from the enclosure, just as we were giving her a walking tour around the perimeter. While Caroline ran to ring for help and I tried, unsuccessfully, to block their exit, Jane distracted them from the hole in the fence by mobile play invitations and vocalizations. Quite a sight!

Once at Gombe, I studied chimpanzee infant development, as planned, following from my graduate studies of preschool-age children. However, the apes' tool use intrigued me, and Jane was kind enough to let me switch to a topic that I've pursued ever since, for more than forty years. This was typical of Jane: if you made a good case, reasonably and sensibly, she'd give you the benefit of the doubt. But among Jane's most basic but crucial traits is being a good listener. In more than four decades, I've never heard her interrupt anyone in conversation. This is remarkable for someone who's spent hours listening to strangers, whether they are hosts in far-flung places or strangers who accost her on airplanes. Who knows how many thousands of hours Jane has spent listening to breathless students describe how she's inspired them, presumably telling her variations on the same story, again and again and again? Yet not only is she impeccably polite, but she actually listens.

Jane Goodall has never had a permanent academic position and so cannot be credited with being anyone's official academic supervisor, but she has crucially influenced so many students, by paying attention and opening doors.

WILLIAM C. MCGREW, professor emeritus of evolutionary primatology at the University of Cambridge, spent forty years chasing chimpanzees from Tanzania to Sénégal and back, having started at Gombe in 1972 and finished there in 2012.

The "Joys" of Frodo

LINDA F. MARCHANT

Jane was walking on the southside trail of Kasekela Stream, and she looked unhappy and worried. The previous evening I'd spent a little time with her when she arrived at Gombe for one of those treasured visits, since most of her time was now taken up with travel and fundraising lectures. Jane's Gombe visits were meant to be relaxing and rejuvenating. Yet here she was coming up the path looking distressed.

This was my first fieldwork at Gombe. I'd come there with Bill McGrew to spend the fall of 1992 studying chimpanzee hand preference, but we also wanted to get a better grasp (hah!) of the hand-use repertoire of wild chimpanzees, and this included tool use. Remarkably, some of the same termite mounds that Bill had seen Kasekela chimpanzees termite-fish in during the early 1970s were still being fished in the 1990s. I'd been doing a walking tour of some of those mounds and had just left an unproductive stakeout at a mound where I had hoped to see chimpanzees termite-fishing. There were some tools around the mound, knuckle prints where they may have prospected, but, alas, no chimps.

Despite Jane's expression, I was all smiles. Then we locked eyes, and she gestured over her shoulder. That's when I saw who was troubling Jane. It was Frodo. He was seventeen years old, coming into his prime, and some said he was the biggest male they'd ever seen at Gombe. He was also a bully who routinely pummeled other chimpanzees as he worked his way up the male hierarchy and dominated the adult females. Lately, Frodo had extended his displays to incorporate fieldworkers, especially the women.

Frodo was right behind Jane, tight-lipped with an intense expression on his face. She told me he'd already hit her, and it looked like we were both in for it. She told me to grab something to hold onto, which was a way to keep from being dragged if a chimpanzee got hold of a leg. I remember wrapping my arms around a puny tree, while I watched Frodo launch himself at Jane. She didn't have time to get hold of a tree. Frodo grabbed her ankle and dragged her into the streambed, and then he turned his attention to me. I was lucky. All I got was a kick in the side, and then he scrambled dramatically away. But I was shaken, and thus shaking as I ran to Jane, asking if she was OK and babbling about "pilo-erection" and "male dominance behavior." Jane picked herself up, dusted herself down, and then proceeded to use a few choice words to describe Frodo and how she felt about him—words best not to put down in print. She also had an amused and patient look on her face, as she reminded me that saying Frodo's hair "bristled" was a perfectly good way to talk about his appearance. Really, who needed to use *piloerection* when we all knew what *bristled* meant? She then said, very wisely I might add, "Let's go find Wilkie. Frodo wouldn't dare act like this around him!" That made perfect sense. Wilkie was the current alpha, and even Frodo was not such a great fool that he would display such behavior around the alpha.

So that's what we did. We made our way on trails while we talked about Gombe and the chimpanzees I'd spent time with since arriving there. She asked how Gremlin was doing, as that was who she'd been looking for when she met Frodo instead. We ended up at camp and sat a while longer—talking about termite fishing and what a problem Frodo was—when pretty soon Wilkie strolled into camp. Safe at last!

I think about that day a lot and remember what Jane taught me. Be brave, be irreverent, and use simple words to describe what you see.

LINDA F. MARCHANT, professor of anthropology at Miami University in Oxford, Ohio, has studied wild chimpanzees and bonobos in Tanzania, Uganda, Sénégal, and the Democratic Republic of the Congo.

To Jane Goodall

CAROL GIGLIOTTI

Dear Jane,

I only met you once, in the early '80s at a reception for an award you were receiving from the Animal Welfare Institute in Washington, DC. I was already committed to animal rights and was a visual artist whose work was about factory farming and vivisection. Now I write, and all my writing is about animals.

After the ceremony, people lined up to talk to you. I joined the line, wanting to tell you how important your work with and for animals was to me. When I finally reached you, you gave me all your attention. In fact,

I was bowled over by your astonishing ability to listen to this person you did not know, and I came away with a desire to foster that same quiet focus in myself. I don't remember what was said, but how I felt when talking to you was something I value to this day.

I have been a teacher for the last thirty years, and I have cultivated that listening ability you taught me in interactions with my students, with animals, and with human friends and family. I want to thank you for allowing me a glimpse into a very different way of being in the world. Your example has given me much joy and satisfaction and has taught me a fruitful path to compassion. It was a huge gift and I thank you for it.

CAROL GIGLIOTTI is a writer, artist, scholar, and activist whose work offers a more comprehensive understanding of creativity through recognizing animal cognition, creativity, consciousness, and agency.

Flying with Jane

JOE DUFF

The air was perfectly smooth as our wheels left the ground and we took off into the early morning stillness. We flew out over a vast area of pristine wetland that is Necedah National Wildlife Refuge. Mist hung over the open marsh like a protective covering, waiting to be unwrapped by the rising sun.

I pointed out two whooping cranes who were foraging hock-deep in the water below. Five feet tall and brilliant white, they stood out like beacons against the earthy tones of mid-September. They were adult birds and the first of their kind to inhabit the wilds of central Wisconsin in over a hundred years. Wary of humans and as wild as their surroundings, they represented the beginning of a reintroduced flock.

Our mission that morning was not to track the birds we had already led by ultralight aircraft to Florida and were now making the trip on their own, but to prepare the next generation for their first migration south. Brooke Pennypacker was the pilot of the other aircraft in our formation that morning, and he launched off followed by our five-month-old whooping cranes, suddenly released from their isolated pen. They climbed out over the marsh on an exercise flight to build their endurance before we headed south. Flying in the chase position, we moved in from behind, and several birds slipped back to fly on the vortices created by our wingtip. Without flapping their wings, they surfed on our wake, practicing their airmanship. Still mottled with the fawn color of youth and bathed in fog-filtered sunlight, they presented a spectacle for Dr. Jane Goodall, my backseat passenger.

When our flight was over, I let Jane out of the aircraft by the side of the runway. As I taxied slowly back to the hangar alone, I glanced back to where the whooping cranes had been flying only minutes before. There was Jane running beside me, just off the wingtip, and flapping her arms like a bird.

I have to admit to pragmatism. I am more likely to concentrate on the mechanics of teaching birds to migrate than the emotional experience of it. There is poetry in flying with birds, but it was Jane who taught me to hear it.

JOE DUFF is the cofounder of Operation Migration. Since 2001 he has worked to reintroduce endangered whooping cranes into their former range using ultralight aircraft.

Lessons in the Wild with Jane

VIRGINIA MORELL

Probably everyone who loves animals has dreamed of going to watch chimpanzees at Gombe in the company of Jane Goodall, and so I could hardly believe my good fortune when she invited me to join her there for a week in 1985. At the time, I was researching *Ancestral Passions,* my book about the Leakey family. Louis Leakey had been Jane's mentor and helped send her to Gombe to study chimpanzees. Jane gave me new and unexpected insights into Louis's personality.

One day during my visit, Jane went to a small aluminum building where bananas were stored. Doling bananas out to the chimpanzees was at that time a way of attracting them out of the forest and into camp, where they could be observed more easily. The banana provisioning was ordinarily done via remote-controlled steel boxes, but, perhaps for my benefit, Jane had decided to give some bananas to the chimps through a barred window in the building. I watched from an adjacent building. Beethoven, a big male with glossy black fur, was the first visitor. With him was a young female chimpanzee, Dilly, an orphan. Beethoven had adopted Dilly, Jane told me later. Beethoven was both Dilly's benefactor, seeing to it that she had enough to eat from the fruiting trees, and her protector, keeping her safe during times of social excitement. But Beethoven's generosity did not extend to sharing bananas.

Jane handed Beethoven an armful of the fruits, and he squatted on the grass in front of the shed and devoured each one. Little Dilly sat close by, watching as each luscious banana slipped down her protector's gullet. Once she reached out a hand to beg, but Beethoven ignored her. Finally, the last banana consumed and his belly full, Beethoven rolled on his back and fell asleep. Dilly sat beside him, grooming his fur.

Jane had watched that little drama from her window. Unbeknownst to Beethoven, though, she had held back one banana. When Dilly happened to glance at her, Jane held up the prized fruit. Normally, a hungry chimpanzee would make a food cry after spotting such a delectable treat. But Dilly stifled any sound. She watched as Jane placed the banana outside the feeding station, away from Beethoven's line of sight. It was as if she and Jane had exchanged a secret, and like a coconspirator, Dilly played her part. She continued grooming the big male while making cooing, lullaby sounds of contentment.

At last Beethoven began to snore—and Dilly quickly and quietly made her way to the hidden banana. She downed it in three bites. Then she stealthily made her way back to Beethoven's side and resumed her grooming and cooing.

When Jane and I met up later, I immediately brought up Dilly's behavior. I was sure that Jane would be as excited as I was, and that soon she would be writing an article for a major scientific journal about how chimpanzees plot and deceive one another. So I was taken aback when she said that she could not write about what we had witnessed. "If I write it up," she explained, "everyone will say, 'Oh, Jane, how silly of you. That's anthropomorphizing.'"

She would be attributing a human mental ability to an animal. But, surely, I protested, these chimpanzees had to be using their minds. Jane nodded. "Yes, it doesn't make much sense to say they aren't thinking or don't have emotions," she said. "Most of us studying animals in the wild see things like this all the time. But we've learned to be careful. We can say, 'If Dilly were a human, we would say she was acting deceitfully.'"

How could a scientist possibly get around this dilemma? I asked. The problem seemed framed in such a way as to forever preclude considering the mind, the mental potential, of another creature. Jane agreed, but she added that because so many researchers were witnessing similar behaviors (and in a variety of species, not just chimpanzees), she thought the science—the study of animal cognition and emotions—would change. "It has to," she said. "It's just a matter of time."

And she was right. In part because of Jane and her careful reportage on the lives of the wild chimpanzees, we now recognize that they—and many other animals—think and feel, have personalities, do things intentionally, and love and laugh and grieve. From Jane, we learned how to begin bridging the gap between *us* and *them*.

VIRGINIA MORELL is an award-winning author of four books, including *Ancestral Passions* and *Animal Wise*. She is a correspondent for *Science* and *National Geographic* and has written for numerous other publications.

What a Great Teacher She Is!

SHADRACK MKOLLE KAMENYA

I grew up in Kigoma, western Tanzania, on the eastern shore of Lake Tanganyika. When I was a kid, we visited the harbor often, and we played in the lake. Often we saw boats carrying white people pulling into the harbor and leaving the harbor. In those times, we knew that there were some *wazungu*—white people—working in Gombe National Park. I am talking about the late 1960s and early 1970s. This was a time when not many white folks came into this land as tourists. Of course, I had no dream or thought then that one day I would be working among them, and we did not see them closely either, to know the individuals. After all, we were kids.

I visited Gombe in 1990 and then had an opportunity to talk to Dr. Jane Goodall at her residence in Dar es Salaam after getting her telephone number from Dr. Anthony Collins. She had invited me to meet with her, but I failed to do that because of my schedule and also because I had a very short time in the country. I had to rush back to school in the United States at the University of Colorado at Boulder.

Then I had an opportunity to see her on the stage in 1992, when she gave a lecture in Denver during one of her regular American lecture tours. Together with Dr. Anthony, Jane invited me to Gombe National Park for my dissertation work, and so in December 1994, I went there.

Soon after that, Dr. Goodall came to Gombe, and so I had the opportunity to meet her and talk to her in person. She extended her welcoming invitation by suggesting I might work with JGI in Gombe once I finished my doctoral research. She said, "Shadrack, you can come and work with us even for three years and then leave if you wish." At the end of 1997, I finally managed to join the JGI family in Gombe and have been there for over fifteen years now.

Dr. Jane has taught me a great deal. Just watching her walking in the forest impresses me. If you walk as she does in the forest, you will not squash any living objects at all. I have also learned not to misuse resources, such as food, putting little on my plate. I have been with her in a plane, watching her wrapping some disposable spoons and forks for further use. I have watched the way she interacts with little ones (kids) and how she interacts with presidents, then how she deals with her colleagues. The world could be so much lovelier if at least 20 percent of the people were more like Jane. I have watched and listened to her stories about how impressed she is with wildlife, from insects to mammals. She is a unique naturalist. Not many in the world are like her, and unfortunately there is no school to train us to be like her. I will continue learning from this great teacher whenever the opportunities come my way.

SHADRACK MKOLLE KAMENYA has been working with the Jane Goodall Institute in Tanzania since 1997 on matters pertaining to chimpanzee research and conservation.

Jane the Teacher

DALE PETERSON

I first met Jane in June 1989, at the home of Geza Teleki in suburban Washington, DC. Geza had once been a student at Jane's research site in Africa, and I had earlier sought him out as a well-known chimp expert. I wanted to write a book about chimpanzees and conservation, and I had asked Geza if he would provide expert advice. He agreed to help, but then he surprised me by offering to introduce me to Jane Goodall. He said she might be interested in coauthoring such a book. I thought, *Terrific!*

When I met her, she seemed smaller and less dramatic than I had expected. She was quiet, in a thoughtful sort of way. Or was she just tired? Geza and I jointly advanced the idea of a coauthorship. She seemed reluctant, saying, "Wouldn't it be just as good if I wrote an introduction to a book you wrote?"

"No," I said, "it wouldn't be the same."

She said, "Let me think about it."

We continued talking, and then, after several minutes passed, she said, "All right. I'll do it." It was characteristic of Jane, I later realized, to make quick decisions about people. Her quick decision about me was the start of a twenty-five-year relationship I've had with one of the world's great primatologists and chimpanzee experts. That relationship would include, for me, the writing or editing of . . . how many books? I'm not sure. We coauthored that first book, but I also wrote or edited several others in which she had an important role, as subject or collaborator or muse.

My brother, who lived and worked in the area, often doubled as my chauffeur when I was in town. After that first meeting, my brother showed up at Geza's house to give me a ride back to his place. Jane was on her way to the National Geographic offices just then, and my brother offered to drive her there, since we were headed in the same direction. On our way there, though, she started talking about suffering chickens, hens in battery cages, free-range eggs, and so on; and I remember looking over at my brother to exchange a furtive glance. I don't know what he was thinking. I was thinking: *Is this lady a little strange?*

I was interested in conservation and primates, but chickens? Only gradually, over the next few months and then years, did I begin to absorb and appreciate more fully Jane's lifelong sensitivity to animals and animal suffering. More immediately, though, this "strange lady" began to teach me other things. For starters, she taught me a good deal about how to write about animals: how to appreciate and express their potential for subjective experience, even when you don't know exactly what it is. She clarified for me the logic of accepting animals as fellow creatures, ones deserving the respect conveyed by personal pronouns identifying *him* and *her* instead of *it, who* and *whose* rather than *that* or *which*—and so on. Animals are not things, and we should stop using language that implies they are.

She also taught me about wild chimpanzees: introducing me to those at Gombe and sending me off to find other chimp communities elsewhere in Africa, thereby giving me the opportunity to see for myself what chimps are like when they're wild and free. It was during those travels in Africa that I also began to understand some of the powerful forces that are pushing all the great apes and most other primates toward extinction. These forces include the bushmeat trade—the commercial hunting of chimps and gorillas and all other wild animals for meat. Thus, another part of my education for the book brought me, in places across the continent, face to face with baby or juvenile chimpanzees chained to trees and junked cars, hidden away and starving in tiny cages, or being cared for in people's houses and in orphanages. Research for that first book with Jane also led me to find chimps outside Africa—behind the bars in biomedical laboratories, for instance, or under the control of Hollywood animal trainers.

After that coauthored book, I turned to a couple of other projects before returning in 1996 to Jane once more. This time, though, she served as both collaborator and subject. The meaning of *subject* should be clear enough: I had decided to write her biography. She was a collaborator in the sense that she gave me free access to everything, including a lifetime's worth of personal letters, roomfuls of filing cabinets bursting with documents and loose papers, a world filled with friends all ready to be interviewed, and family (mother, father, sister, aunt, son, niece, grandchildren, first husband) all grist for the tape recorder. Possibly the oddest thing I noticed, in my ten years biographicizing this one person, is that she never once asked to see what I was writing. When the typescript was finally done and ready for publication, I thought it would be a simple courtesy to let her have a look, and so she did read it at that point. She asked for a few corrections of factual errors. Nothing else. So what I concluded about Jane is that she is among the least controlling people I have ever met.

Jane has taught me so many things. But by *taught*, I really mean something more subtle and yet more effective than the word usually connotes. I've never had the impression that she was actually teaching me or instructing me about anything. No, she taught without *teaching*. She taught through example. She enabled discoveries to happen. She alerted one to possibilities. She altered an opinion through a few words thoughtfully expressed. And it has been through her quiet teaching that I came to think about animal suffering in broader terms. Her example was an important part of my becoming a vegetarian, and her influence and inspiration have helped keep me writing about animals and animal issues over the last quarter century.

DALE PETERSON is the author of *Jane Goodall: The Woman Who Redefined Man*, the only full biography of Jane; the editor of her two-volume autobiography in letters; and her coauthor for *Visions of Caliban: On Chimpanzees and People*.

How Jane Goodall Saved My Life

GLORIA GROW

Back in 1998, several months after the Fauna Foundation opened and the first chimpanzee residents arrived, there was an escape. The chimps we had rescued were ex-research chimps: battered, betrayed, angry, and scared. I was scared too, and in fact, everything I had ever been told about escapes was terrifying.

Then a very powerful and athletic eight-year-old male named Binky got out of his enclosure. You might imagine young chimpanzees to be small and adorable, and nothing about his name or his age might seem scary—certainly not a threat. Except for one thing: he had been locked behind bars his whole life, born in the research lab for the sole purpose of being an experimental tool for drug testing. He had been torn from his mother, lost many of his family members, witnessed countless acts of cruelty on his cellmates, and seen the humans of his world darting and shooting fellow creatures. He was also eighty pounds of pure chimp muscle, which is, pound for pound, much stronger than human muscle.

Binky did not break out or open the locks himself. I left the door open, much to the amazement of the two people with me in the chimp house that evening. Human error. The days were long and grueling, caring for this newly found family of mine, and I was tired. I made a mistake, a bad one. Suddenly, everything changed, and I was terrified. In the building with me that day were a young woman volunteer from the Jane Goodall Institute and a 250-pound man who foolishly considered himself more ferocious and scary than young Binky.

The young woman escaped into the closet. The man decided he would find a way to get Binky back into his enclosure. His only insights about handling chimp escapes had been learned from the technicians at the lab the chimpanzees came from, where the usual methods for handling out-of-control chimps ranged from darting them with a tranquilizer gun to threatening them with a big scary object or spraying them with a fire extinguisher. Or, if all else failed, killing them. Control was the important common factor of those methods.

Binky had been quietly exploring the building, visiting his friends, taking smoothies off the counter—basically, going about his business. That changed when he saw the big man with the metal bar and fire extinguisher. He stood upright, began to swagger, arms in the air, flailing, ready to attack. Bang! He started pushing over everything in his way. His hair stood on end, his face changed, lips pursed, and he suddenly looked enormous. Nothing was going to stop him. Nothing.

When the man saw him coming, he had just enough time to rush into the bathroom and shut the door. Binky banged on the door loud and hard three times, and then he left and went banging on the closet where the young woman was hiding. Again, three bangs. While this was going on, I was still out of sight, around the corner, staying calm, not getting involved, and not aggravating him further. I began placing goodies for him in his enclosure, hoping he might return, and then wondering what else I could do. At that point, I remembered something I had learned from Jane.

A few nights earlier I had been watching television when an early Jane Goodall documentary was aired. I had seen it many times before, but now with the newly opened sanctuary on my mind, I watched with new eyes. I had never quite appreciated just what this woman was doing. There she was: petite, beautiful, deep in the forests of Africa with some of the most intelligent and incredibly strong beings on the planet. She walked among the chimpanzees, observed them, sat nearby as they worked out their differences. Some, when they stood upright, were almost as tall as she was. Most seemed to weigh more than she did. And certainly all of them were far, far stronger than she could ever hope to be.

Never before had I appreciated what she was doing. Nor had I come close to understanding how dangerous it was—until I was face to face with a free chimpanzee: a research chimpanzee, moreover, one who had been tortured by humans from birth. Not my friend. Not close to me in any way. Just a scared chimpanzee now separated from his family, possibly thinking we would hurt him to get him back inside.

Everything I had learned from the lab vanished from my mind. I turned my thoughts to Jane in the documentary, remembering what she did, how calm she was, how slowly she walked among the chimps, how gently she spoke to them, and how she kept her head down and her body in a nonthreatening posture. I thought about how peaceful and calm and unobtrusive she was among those who could have, in a moment, torn her to pieces. But they didn't, not even those who didn't know her. After all, she had been a complete stranger to them in the beginning, and yet she lived and shared space with them: our cousins, our kin, walking with them, alongside them, not in front, not behind.

I tried to do what she did. I made myself calm. I walked like I knew where I was going and continued about my business, ignoring Binky even after he scared the 250-pound man with the metal bar and fire extinguisher out of the building, leaving me alone with only the young woman hidden in the closet.

Binky must have been relieved that there was no longer a threat. He quickly calmed down, happily following me around for the drinks and goodies I was leaving out. After an hour or so of freedom, he retreated back to his enclosure on his own, content to have had a walk around, a visit with the others, and a chance to eat lots of bubble gum.

Inspired by meeting Washoe, the world's first chimpanzee to learn American Sign Language, GLORIA GROW wanted to find out what she could do to help. She heard Jane speak about the need to build chimpanzee sanctuaries, so with Richard Allan she established the Fauna Foundation in Canada.

Thank You for Being Daring and Caring

HAMID R. HOSSAINI

Dear Jane,

I joined your online hang-out birthday party and watched your interview with National Geographic. When you emphatically reminded the interviewer, twice, that animals are "he" and "she," not "it," I reached for the phone and cancelled my contract with the bee terminator!

Honeybees have been living in the old chimney of our house for years. All the residents of this house have had multiple gifts of sting when on hot days hundreds of bees would come down the chimney, like Santa, to visit. And we let them be. Recently, though, due to some complaints and the beeswax and honey melting down the chimney as a result of extreme summer heat, we had to hire—as a legal necessity—authorized professionals to get rid of the bees.

As I watched your interview and saw you protest about animals being referred to as "it," I could not bear the thought of eliminating those 60,000 to 80,000 individuals in my chimney. I took the affair in hand, risking legal troubles, and started to alert the bees that, sadly, they should leave and that they were no longer welcomed by the neighborhood. With a few tricks, such as changing the draft in the chimney and enlarging the passages to the chamber where the honeycombs and hives were hanging, I let them know that it was best for them to find a new home. Hoping that I could be of further assistance, I then carefully took a few thousand of them to the parkland, just fifty meters away from the house, where there are hundreds of tall trees and miles of wildflower beds. In two weeks, they were all gone (I hope to the parkland), except for a few hundred scouts from other colonies who had come to take over the vacated palace.

As I climbed the chimney to clear the melted wax in order to discourage the new bees from hanging around, a few of them sat on my bee-proof veil. A brighter and bigger one sat closer to my eyes and nose, and I was reminded of David Greybeard and you. I want to believe that the bee near my eyes was the queen who thanked me for not eliminating her and terminating her Nation. As they paraded to their new home and I looked at the empty throne, I said, "Thank you, Jane."

Thank you for reinforcing in all of us the care and concern for all beings. I would like to believe that the queen sent her gratitude and her message to you. Thank you, Jane, for being caring and daring!

HAMID R. HOSSAINI has served the United Nations in areas affected by war and natural disasters, and on issues related to the survival of women and children. He is one of the architects of the 1990 World Summit for Children and has helped introduce Roots & Shoots into refugee camps in Africa, India, Australia, and Iran.

JANE AS NATURALIST

As a child, Jane was unusually mature. As an adult, she is remarkably child-like, fully connected to her childhood self. Reaching out to and being with children is her passion and identity, central to who she is and where she's going. She was and still is a "young naturalist" at heart—an idea expressed in "Two Simple Questions" by Jeanne McCarty. That's the emotional logic of Jane Goodall's young naturalists' club known as Roots & Shoots.

Roots & Shoots began in 1991 when, at her home in Dar es Salaam, Jane met with a group of young Tanzanians interested in learning about nature and frustrated that nature and the environment were not part of their normal education. In this section's second essay, Greg MacIsaac, who was a teacher in Dar es Salaam at that time, describes the club's modest beginning—a tiny seed planted among a small group of students in Tanzania. But then the seed was watered, and it began to grow. MacIsaac was one of the inspired gardeners who helped, not only during the early days in Tanzania but also later on, in China. Rick Asselta, another gardener, worked with Roots & Shoots in Tanzania, then in New England, 140 American universities, and on to Latin America and the Caribbean. Mie Horiuchi Strunden helped plant Roots & Shoots in Japan and then worked with schoolchildren in Uganda. From Colombia, South America, we have gardener Ybeth Pinzón's story. From Oklahoma, Pam O'Halloran-Blevins describes the growth of Roots & Shoots at Riverfield Country Day Middle School. And, from the state of Washington, Jonathan Lucero tells how Jane persuaded him to get involved as a volunteer.

With the help of a thousand similarly inspired gardeners, the club has grown, spread its roots, and reached for the light with shoots, and in that fashion has broken through barriers and grown remarkably since those early days. Today Roots & Shoots clubs can be found around the globe, and the movement has also expanded to include people of many cultures, situations, and ages, all united in the ideal of healing the earth and the hope of overcoming barriers that separate people from animals and from the environment. Yes, you don't have to be a child or even young to be a "young naturalist." The inclusiveness of Roots & Shoots can be illustrated partly by the positive thoughts and wishes coming from Richard Mora of the Boulder County Jail Roots & Shoots chapter in Colorado.

From Italy, meanwhile, Daniela de Donno Mannini, president and executive director of JGI Italy, describes her participation in a Roots & Shoots photography project at the Nisida Island Prison in Naples. From Beijing, China, comes the testimony of one early Roots & Shoots member, James Tsou-Wang, who has become a passionate and committed environmentalist. Another Roots & Shoots graduate, Caitlin Kara, describes joining forces with Shadrach Meshach, a club member in Tanzania, to form the nonprofit organization My Two Hands, which helps refugees in sub-Saharan Africa.

Good teaching rewards the teacher as much as the student. Renée Gunther, formerly a teacher for twenty-eight years in a middle school in the Bronx, New York, describes how Roots & Shoots changed her life in specific ways: led to a "huge promotion," raised her pension, and enabled her to overcome her phobia of speaking in public. And from Los Angeles, California, John Zavalney describes how meeting Jane and becoming a Roots & Shoots organizer transformed his life in some possibly less practical but potentially more encompassing ways.

—D. P.

Two Simple Questions

JEANNE MᶜCARTY

"Tell me about your childhood. Tell me about your relationship with animals."

Those were the only two questions Dr. Jane Goodall asked me in my job interview for the director of the Jane Goodall Institute's Roots & Shoots program.

I still remember sitting in my living room, anxiously awaiting her call from Tanzania. I'd already made it through multiple rounds of interviews. I'd been over every work experience. I'd researched and thought through my answers to any conceivable questions. I knew I was ready. I couldn't have been more wrong.

Dr. Jane almost stumped me by asking those two unexpected questions—and now that I think back on it, they weren't technically questions.

But suddenly, this call I'd been on edge about stopped being an interview. I found myself talking with Dr. Jane about catching tadpoles in the creek behind my house. And her peaceful, warm, and inquisitive voice on the line got me to remember and relate things I hadn't thought about in years. She invited me to sit beside her imaginatively and share in a moment. I was so at ease. Apparently, she felt as comfortable with me as I did with her, and for the next eight years and more, I had the honor and privilege to work with Dr. Jane and her many friends to grow her youth program. But I've often looked back on those two questions—or instructions—and asked myself why they mattered.

The one about animals is more obvious, but asking about my childhood surprised me. Now, after spending time with her, then spending time running a nonprofit of my own and becoming a mother, I realize just how important childhood is for all of us. Through her, I learned that while our childhoods make us who we are, we, in turn, can also make our childhoods last and can keep them alive for as long as we wish. Dr. Jane would never hesitate to lie down in soft grass on a sunny day, find the beauty in a feather that happened to float across her path, or carry a child's stuffed toy monkey (the legendary Mr. H) with her around the world.

Now that I have become a mother, my son, Will, is my daily reminder to nurture that sense of wonder and compassion: in him and in myself. On a recent walk to school, every icicle fascinated him. He told me, "These are the first icicles I've ever seen!" Although we were running late, I took the time to let him examine and enjoy each one: the way they encased the trees, the various shapes they made, their cold, smooth slickness, and the crackle and crunch of those that fell. I thought they were wonderful too.

Dr. Jane reminds us to nurture curiosity in our children and in ourselves. She keeps childhood—that special time of excitement, awe, and appreciation of this amazing world—with her, and she awakens it in others. Keeping in touch with our childhood is the most basic, the simplest, and the truest part of who we are and what we do. Dr. Jane helped me discover that it was still inside me.

JEANNE MCCARTY was vice president and director of Jane Goodall's Roots & Shoots for over eight years and has more than two decades of experience in education and conservation. She is the executive director of REAL School Gardens.

Why Does Jane Goodall Inspire Me?

GREG MacISAAC

In 1991, in Dar es Salaam, Tanzania, I was asked to help out in a week-long celebration of Jane Goodall's thirty years of work at Gombe. Following the celebrations, she invited a group of students back to her house on the beach in Mikocheni. Some of the Tanzanian students within this group were complaining that they didn't learn much about environmental issues in their schools, while their communities seemed to lack any environmental awareness. Jane suggested that they organize themselves into a young naturalists' group. She said that in order to raise awareness, you have to be active and set an example.

By the following week, the group had organized a beach cleanup and then marched through the streets of Dar es Salaam and along the ocean road. Jane, along with Tanzania's minister of energy, led the march, attracting hundreds of participants along the way. It was one of those rare Gandhi moments, where one felt inspired and intuitively knew that something good was happening.

After the beach had been cleaned up, the restaurant across the road from the beach saw its business flourish because more people went to the beach. So the restaurant owners installed permanent refuse containers near the road. The beach stayed clean, and everyone benefited. From then on, I wanted to be part of the organization Jane had started. It had taken the name Roots & Shoots and embraced the mission of inspiring young people to be activists on behalf of animals, people, and the environment.

By 1992, Roots & Shoots (R&S) was taking hold and beginning to flourish in Tanzania. Jane was working with a group of Tanzanian students in developing the R&S philosophy and program. At the time, I was a teacher at the International School of Tanganyika. When I went to the East African International Teacher's Conference in Nairobi, I took the opportunity to spread the word of a new environmental education program under the Jane Goodall Institute umbrella.

I arrived with some printed brochures and was given five minutes at the podium to talk about all the great things happening in Dar es Salaam with the R&S group. And when I told the audience that Jane would visit their school if they started a group, everyone wanted a copy of the brochure. Then, when I left Tanzania for China in 1994, Jane said to me, "Greg, if you start a group in China, I'll come and visit you." After I started a Roots & Shoots group in Beijing, Jane made her first visit to China.

When we met, she said to me, "Greg, I told you I would come!" Now, after Jane has made more than a dozen visits, Roots & Shoots is actually the leading environmental education program in mainland China. And when I look back at that early start of this children's club in Tanzania—such a modest beginning—and see what has since transpired, with Roots & Shoots established in 120 countries around the world, I ask myself the question: why does Jane Goodall inspire me? But I really don't know the answer. All I know is that something good happened.

GREG MACISAAC has been working in international education for the past thirty years. He became involved in Roots & Shoots in 1991 and is a founding director of the Jane Goodall Institute of China.

What Would Jane Do?

RICK ASSELTA

Dear Jane,

About twenty years ago I was fighting off cancer while working at a high school for troubled young people. Then I met you.

Several weeks later, I was off to Tanzania to help reforest a nation and establish sports programs for thousands of disabled and marginalized Tanzanians. Then it was back to the United States to establish Roots & Shoots in New England, then at 140 American universities, then in Latin America and the Caribbean. You really know how to keep a person busy!

We have been friends, partners, troublemakers, dreamers, and doers of the possible and impossible. We've shared each other's families, frustrations, and joys. We used marathons and wheelchairs to help moms, dads, and kids lead better lives and to comfort the discouraged. And I know you've prevented at least two young people from committing suicide—two lives that are now enriching our world.

We've driven through raging Panamanian rivers, dealt with the Tanzanian bombings, organized Peace Day at the Twin Towers in New York, kicked soccer balls with Kofi Annan at the UN, and told jokes on moonlit nights on the beach in Tanzania and on my farm in Puerto Rico. And we brought your message to countless children and adults that they can make a difference.

Anytime I find myself in a difficult situation, I usually approach it by asking, what would Jane do?

RICK ASSELTA, Roots & Shoots program coordinator in the United States, Tanzania, Latin America, and the Caribbean, is an organic farmer in Puerto

Rico, a cancer survivor, and a disabled athlete who has competed in thirty-two marathons.

Follow Your Dreams

MIE HORIUCHI STRUNDEN

I hardly watch TV. But on that day fourteen years ago in Oregon, I, a young international student from Japan, happened to switch on the TV to take a break from my studies and came across the PBS series *Reason for Hope*. It was the very first time I "met" Jane Goodall and learned about her life and how threatened chimpanzees are in the wild. I still remember my feelings during the program: awe, inspiration, and a determination to help.

An intuition or inner voice told me to pick up the phone. I called the Jane Goodall Institute, which at that time was based in Maryland. I told the receptionist, "I just watched *Reason for Hope* and felt strongly inspired to support Dr. Goodall. How can I be your intern?" The receptionist said, "Well, you can submit your cover letter and résumé, but first of all, do you live in the area?" I said, "No." She replied, "Are you going to come here alone without having a place to live, not knowing anyone? What are you going to do?" And I said, "I will find a way!" A few months later, after persistent e-mail and phone calls, I stood at the doorstep of the Jane Goodall Institute on the first day of my internship. A few months after that, I was offered a job as its communications coordinator.

My work at the Institute led me to ask, What can I do to make a difference? The answer was to help develop Roots & Shoots. I have an abiding passion for this program, which asks young people to engage in service on behalf of people, animals, and the environment. My passion led me to travel many times back home to Japan to meet and work with inspiring people who truly care about the future of our children and the chimpanzees. Through our joint effort, the Jane Goodall Institute was established in Japan in 2001. Since then, Jane and I have had many fun and rewarding trips there.

Jane says: "If you want to achieve something, work hard for it, never give up, and you will find a way." That message keeps echoing. In 2004, one of my biggest dreams came true. I flew to Uganda to work in schools located in villages surrounding the chimpanzee habitat at Kibale National Park. Living in a chimpanzee forest taught me more than I could have possibly imagined about the realities of chimpanzee conservation. Every day I worked with my Ugandan colleagues and the local children, trying to better understand and live in harmony with the chimpanzees. We worked hard to understand each other, understand the issues, and find solutions. The children decided to form their own Roots & Shoots groups and then began to take action. They performed an environmental play, built nurseries for indigenous trees, organized a cleanup around the school, and much more. It was an intense year full of inspiration, and it moved me to pursue a master's degree in international development the following year.

"Each one of us is unique and has the potential to make a positive difference in this world." That is the message from Jane that moved me and keeps on doing so. Now I am a mother of two children, and as I pass this important message on to my children, it means even more and brings me new perspectives. Even today, my experience with Jane, the Institute, and the children in Uganda form the backbone of my life, and will continue to do so.

MIE HORIUCHI STRUNDEN helped found the Jane Goodall Institute in Japan and has worked with Roots & Shoots there and elsewhere. She also worked with schoolchildren near the chimpanzee project at Kibale Forest, Uganda, and is a yoga teacher.

Jane's Magic: I've Seen It Happen

YBETH PINZÓN

Today is one of those days that will end with the feeling of so-much-to-do-where-to-begin? Almost breathless, I remember Jane's words, take a deep breath, and bring to mind her interior peace during those crazy days of her visit to Colombia. Then I retrace the steps in my life since I first met Jane in Panamá. Her strength spreads like seeds from a great ancestral tree.

Dr. Jane Goodall inspired me to begin a Roots & Shoots school that I hope will honor her hard work. I've seen what a difference can be made when hope is planted in a child's heart. I deeply believe that the kids who come to my school develop a respect for other people, animals, and the environment. We go every Wednesday to the beach. Kids pick up plastic and then say to me, "Miss, I've just saved a turtle!" And I feel so proud because I know I'm educating students for life and not just for good grades. In this school we make it clear that every individual matters and can make a difference.

I first met Jane through Roots & Shoots, and I fell in love with the program. My daughter and I shared her ideas with the Latin American leaders I knew. When she came to my country, she engaged everybody who heard her. I think a big part of her magic is that rather than being *against* things, she instead is always standing up for a good cause—while always being honest, direct, patient, joyful, and respectful. So many lessons and so many deep transformations in only five days in Colombia. When she came, I witnessed the power of positive persuasion and inspiration. I understood that many good things happen when you touch someone's heart. Now I know, and I'm proud to say that I'm part of this big family that is working toward change and I am committed to passing on her words and following her example.

Thanks, Jane, for the magic. I saw it happen.

YBETH PINZÓN met Jane Goodall at a Panama Summit in 2012. Since then she has committed herself to the Roots & Shoots program.

Happy Eightieth, Dr. Jane

PAM O'HALLORAN-BLEVINS

Dr. Jane,

Happy eightieth, from your friends in Oklahoma! Boy! I remember celebrating several birthdays with you, starting about twenty-five years ago at a National Science Teacher's Association Convention. What wonderful memories we've shared in that quarter century. I remember when you visited Hale High School in 1989 to dedicate the Ecology Club outdoor classroom to Tim O'Halloran and his students. You were in Tulsa working with the Tulsa Zoo on the primate exhibit, but you found the time to come to our school and greet over a hundred or more elementary, middle school, and high school students and faculty. We squeezed everyone into the gymnasium as you pant-hooted your greeting. The outdoor nature center must have been a hit, because you asked Tim and me to share the nature center blueprints so that you could take them back to England to your own elementary school. It was a beginning of a great friendship and several wonderful events we were able to collaborate on. At the time, Tim and I had created a science club called Keepers of the Earth for our kindergarten through high school students. Our membership card had three conditions.

In order to become a member of the Keepers of the Earth you must:

1. Be kind to animals,
2. Be kind to the environment,
3. Be kind to others.

Does that sound familiar? The seeds for the Roots & Shoots philosophy were already planted and had begun to bloom! Then came the amazing R&S campouts at Reed Oppenheimer's ranch, followed by R&S summits in Oklahoma, Colorado, Arizona, and Canada; educational workshops for science and environmental conventions; and the unforgettable R&S retreats on Whidbey Island outside Seattle with Chitcus and Uncle from Greenland; and lastly, the wonderful dedication ceremony you led at the Riverfield High School Tim O'Halloran started in 2005. Together, we have lit many candles, toasted the clouds, shared many visions, and prayed for many others around the world. You will always be in my heart and mind. Your friendship and leadership still inspire me today, as I coordinate a middle school Roots & Shoots club at Riverfield Country Day School. Our students and teachers have built and maintain gardens and nature areas, care for classroom and barnyard animals, coordinate campus recycling, volunteer for Special Olympics, work with disabled and homeless people in the community, and volunteer for many other campus and community events.

You are our inspiration! You are my hero!

PAM O'HALLORAN-BLEVINS taught elementary grades in public schools for many years. She currently teaches middle school science and leads the Roots & Shoots program at the Riverfield Country Day School in Tulsa, Oklahoma.

A Way to Be Involved

JONATHAN LUCERO

I first met Jane when I was working with the American Indian movement. We had mutual friends. We realized we had a lot in common. I had been going to East Africa for a couple of years. I too loved primates. Soon every time she came to the Bay Area, I would receive an e-mail a few weeks before. I accompanied her to Casa Grande High School in Petaluma, California, to honor the students who had done such good work with Roots & Shoots. At that time only a few schools in California were doing the program. Once in a while Jane would ask me what I was doing, meaning what was I doing for the future generations. For a long time I was able to sidestep the answer.

Then Jane figured I should be doing more. First she tried flattery. "Oh, Jonathan, you have such a gift for storytelling." I knew sooner or later she would get me. Then I received an e-mail asking me to meet her at the Marin Vets Hall in San Rafael, my hometown. Jane was going to speak to a very large gathering of people interested in Roots & Shoots. I met her beforehand, met several dignitaries, was very impressed, and at one point said to myself, What am I doing here? Soon a young man came to escort us to our very special seats. As Jane came out to speak to the thousand or so people, everyone rose to their feet, clapping forever. Jane began to speak, and it was silent.

Mind you, I was still on the fence about getting involved with the

Roots & Shoots program. Jane had always said there was a place for me somewhere. About half an hour into her presentation, she told the crowd that if anyone needed more information they had someone right here in San Rafael they could ask. With that, she had a spotlight focus on my seat and promptly introduced me to the entire audience.

So I found something I could do to help. I have spoken for Jane many times to schools, from first grade to high school. As usual, Jane was right. I found a way to be involved.

JONATHAN LUCERO, an Apache native from New Mexico, works with Ingrid Nyberg organizing a Roots & Shoots project at the Frantz Coe Elementary School in Seattle, Washington.

We, the People

RICHARD MORA

To Dr. Jane Goodall:

We, the people of Boulder County, would like to wish you a very happy eightieth birthday.

We also would like to thank you for your hard work as an animal activist and a Messenger of Peace for the United Nations.

We, the people, appreciate all the footage and study you presented on the day-to-day lives of the wild chimpanzees in Africa.

Thank you for organizing and implementing the Roots & Shoots program and for all the inspiration you have brought to people, families, and organizations around the world.

You have built a firm foundation with Roots & Shoots. Through that organization we, the people, can seek, discover, and be a part of new ways to grow, learn, and take action to improve the world.

Thank you, Dr. Goodall.

RICHARD MORA is a member of the Jane Goodall Roots & Shoots project at Boulder County Jail in Colorado.

Magic Jane
DANIELA DE DONNO MANNINI

It is the day I have awaited for so long. My colleagues and I planned every single minute of the day weeks ago. It is the last phase of a Roots & Shoots project: time to communicate results, congratulate, and celebrate. This project is particularly delicate and a big responsibility for JGI. We are in Naples—or, to be more precise, we are on the enchanting Nisida Island in the Naples Gulf.

We cross a bridge to reach the police station. Here we show identification and explain where we are going. Nisida is, in fact, a prison island for youths convicted of serious crimes. Many have been laborers for the local mafia, the *camorra*. They are young men who had the misfortune to be born in areas controlled by the camorra. Between fourteen and twenty years old, they are used to thinking that they have no alternatives. And yet they do not want to hear or believe that they are victims of the mafia.

The director of the prison has opened the Nisida doors to Jane Goodall's Roots & Shoots program. Thanks to Marc Bekoff, JGI can claim more than ten years' experience with R&S projects in jails, but the program at Nisida is a first for JGI in Italy.

Francesca, Maria, Marcello, and I have done a great job with the Nisida youth, who join the program on a volunteer basis. After our first presentation, eighteen out of twenty decided to join. I think they were curious to hear about this crazy woman who dreamed of studying African animals. The director and magistrates of the penitentiary are proud of these young prisoners and their work. In the first five months of the program, they did so well searching for beauty on their prison island that the project even received a medal from the president of the Italian Republic, Giorgio Napolitano.

But today is a day to enjoy, after months of hard work. Today is the opening for the Nisida R&S group's photograph exhibition, "Shapes of Beauty: Each Person Is a Project." Only a few of our young men can participate in the opening because the exhibition room is just before the steel portal—beyond which is freedom—and they are not allowed to gather there as a whole group. Nevertheless, some are there, and the others will have their turns later on.

The event starts with a video message from Jane, and her famous chimpanzee call welcomes the young prisoners and the public and press. We continue with the ceremony.

One of the young participants, Nicolai, explains why he liked the R&S course so much. He says, "It has changed my life." "And what did you learn, Nicolai?" the journalist asks, hoping for more. "That another life is possible. That I can have other opportunities in my life, other dreams if I work hard and don't give up."

The press conference is ending, and I thank everyone for their participation. Amid the applause, we hear "Uhu, Uhu, Uhu. Uhu, Uhuuu." Jane is greeting us once again in chimpanzee language, but no technician has pushed the *play* button on the video machine. The public and journalists believe it was part of the plan: a final, conclusive chimp greeting to end the press conference. Francesca, Maria, Marcello, and I look at each other bewildered and conclude it's magic Jane!

DANIELA DE DONNO MANNINI is the founder and executive director of JGI Italy.

Roots & Shoots in China

JAMES TSOU-WANG

When in 1994 my fourth-grade teacher began telling the class stories of his time working with Dr. Jane Goodall, I had no idea that a lifelong passion had just begun. But before I knew it, I had signed up to work with the first Roots & Shoots group in China.

Despite growing up in central Beijing, my interest in the environment had already been high, yet the watershed moment that led me to pursue a career in environmental protection happened when I first heard Dr. Jane Goodall speak. Since then I have studied and worked all over the world, pursuing ways to help improve the environment. Throughout this time, the key message that Dr. Goodall taught me, that every individual can make a difference, continues to guide me and my pursuit to help improve the environment.

As I study environmental protection at graduate school, I continue to expand my links with the Roots & Shoots and Jane. In 2012, I worked in the Roots & Shoots Beijing Office on a wetlands education program in coordination with the Western Academy of Beijing (WAB). As I work at the wetlands WAB project and elsewhere in Beijing, I can still recall my very first days working with Roots & Shoots. I feel a sense of pride at how far it has come—and also a sense of determination when I consider how far we still must go.

JAMES TSOU-WANG discovered his life's passion for environmental protection after meeting Jane in Beijing and working with the first Roots & Shoots group in China.

Together We Can Do So Much

CAITLIN KARA

I came of age at a time of great tension and uncertainty. It was 1996. I was nine, and I started to consider the larger world: the First Congolese War, global warming, and laboratory animal experimentation. For me, the future hung in the balance of vulnerability. Feelings of a new despondency cast darkness across a light of hope that, just months before, had been kindled with the cease-fire in Bosnia and Chechnya and the reign of peace in Sarajevo.

At this time of doubt, Jane Goodall inspired me and thousands of other young people, becoming a source of strength in a time of weakness. Through her Roots & Shoots program, I and thousands of others were empowered by the belief that every individual matters, every individual has a role to play, every individual makes a difference. Those who joined Roots & Shoots soon realized that working together, we could do so much for the environment, animals, and humankind.

The more involved I became in Roots & Shoots, the more aware I grew of the interrelated structure of our world and my purpose in it. I became an advocate for animal rights and a steward of the earth. In 2001, I stumbled upon my destiny when Jane shared with me her knowledge of the refugee crisis in sub-Saharan Africa and encouraged me to become involved. As a result, Shadrach Meshach (a Roots & Shoots brother from Tanzania) and I established a nonprofit for refugees that aimed at advocacy, education, protection, and environmental sustainability. We aim to help them rebuild their lives and to empower them through Roots & Shoots.

This is the idea that Roots & Shoots so beautifully illustrates: that each individual has worth and can contribute to the worth of all. This idea of interdependence has supported an entire generation of young people in understanding that we share an emotional, ecological, and moral responsibility to all living things: to the environment, animals, humankind.

The challenges we face today are inseparable. Ending displacement for the world's refugees cannot be separated from eradicating war and initiating peace. Initiating peace is inseparable from supporting displaced people and enabling them to return to their fields and pastures, their villages and schools—which are the roots of hope and possibility. Returning the displaced to those roots is inseparable from teaching them to tend the earth and care for her inhabitants compassionately. Tending to our earth with compassion is inseparable from protecting the wild and free and *keeping* them wild and free.

At this moment, the present hangs in the balance of vulnerability. No single person is capable of overcoming these challenges alone. But, yes, together we can do so much. Jane's words, "Roots that creep underground and make a firm foundation," could describe the global village of resolute individuals that she has created who, because of her vision and passion, are shoots that can "break open brick walls" to make our world a better place.

CAITLIN KARA, songwriter, singer, and instrumentalist, is also the founder and CEO of the nonprofit My Two Hands, which supports refugees and displaced persons of sub-Saharan Africa. She has been a member of Roots & Shoots since the age of seven.

Roots & Shoots Changed My Life

RENÉE GUNTHER

Dear Jane,

It all began when I attended your lecture to New York City teachers. I was in my twenty-eighth year of teaching middle school in the Bronx when I first learned of Roots & Shoots. The theme of my science classes was appreciation, respect, and compassion for all living things. You added the special ingredient of putting our compassion into action. My teaching strategy changed, and I watched my students soar.

As our projects became successful and gained some degree of fame, or notoriety, I was confronted more and more by my shyness. We were asked to speak at Fordham University, to the community school board, to the superintendent, and at various faculty meetings. This meant I had to come out of my comfortable place behind classroom walls and speak publicly— my greatest fear.

At the end of the school year, however, I was offered a position as director of the program Middle School Quality Initiatives for the Bronx. My students' Roots & Shoots projects had changed me! This was a huge promotion. It raised my pension considerably, but most importantly, I overcame my nemesis: my fear of public speaking.

After I retired, I felt lost with all that free time. Teaching is my passion, and a part of me felt empty without it. Once again, I embraced Roots & Shoots, and now I speak comfortably at faculty meetings and in classes. It is an honor to represent our program. Last year was my most successful. Forty-eight classes in Tucson became members. This year my greatest accomplishment was signing up a class on the Tohono O'odham Nation Reservation.

Two highlights of my beloved career involve you.

One was standing inside a giant tree with you and my four students who were chosen to attend the 1999 Oregon Youth Summit. You were talking about saving the forests of the world, and I became very teary-eyed thinking, Here I am inside this magnificent tree with my children from the Bronx and *Jane Goodall*. This was a pinnacle of my career.

The other extremely moving experience was when you presented me with the 2011 Excellence in Education Award from JGI.

RENÉE GUNTHER considers herself fortunate to be alive because her parents were both Holocaust survivors. Her occupation as a teacher in the Bronx led to many successful experiences.

Inspiration, Mentor, and Friend
JOHN ZAVALNEY

From the moment Dr. Jane Goodall sat next to me, as she introduced Roots & Shoots to an inner-city school in 1996, my world was forever altered. A few months later I was in Tanzania for three months as an R&S volunteer and living in Dr. Goodall's home in Dar es Salaam. In Dar, I helped plan and celebrate Roots & Shoots Week, met with and helped support current groups, tried recruiting new schools, and at last spent a week at Gombe going into the forest to observe chimpanzees.

Once I had an opportunity to speak with Jane, made a connection with her, and then received a directive from her, I felt empowered and committed. Dr. Goodall wanted Roots & Shoots to work in the inner city, and I felt a personal quest to do my best to make this happen. Once I got home from Tanzania, therefore, my wife, Darlene, and I helped form the Los Angeles R&S steering committee. The committee produced an activities and curriculum plan, and it hosted several Goodall events and promoted Roots & Shoots at environmental and educational fairs and conferences. Because of my involvement with the program, I was now reaching out to thousands of students and many teachers beyond my classroom and school. Representing and promoting Dr. Goodall and her Roots & Shoots program has opened so many doors and given me opportunities I never could have imagined.

After she called my home and told us about her selection as a United Nations Messenger of Peace, we were given a new charge. Jane envisioned enough giant peace doves being flown on the United Nations Day of Peace that they could be seen from outer space. We began learning how to make the giant doves. Traveling to Roots & Shoots clubs with sheets donated by hotels and hospitals, Darlene and I helped students and teachers build hundreds of giant doves. For Dr. Goodall's seventieth birthday, the Los Angeles steering committee put together a celebration at the Huntington Gardens that featured the largest giant peace dove parade in the world.

Following that event, Darlene and I spearheaded United Nations Day of Peace events in Los Angeles, starting in San Pedro with a hundred or so participants and eighteen doves. We then moved to Griffith Park, with support from LA City councilman Tom LeBonge. Those events featured dozens of environmental vendors, hundreds of participants, and special celebrity hosts and musicians. The power of Jane allowed us to bring together over 10,000 people at one event and to have the largest giant dove parade in the world eight years in a row, each one bigger than the last, while celebrating bringing peace to the environment, animals, and the human community through Roots & Shoots. During this period, I also served on the school district's service board, working to design the graduation requirement of a community service project. Roots & Shoots became a partner in that, providing environmental projects for students to complete.

Today, Roots & Shoots helps provide service learning projects across the nation. How amazing that my passionate volunteer work became part of my regular job! These events not only changed our lives; they also inspired thousands to make a difference. How powerful is that?

It is hard to put into words how Jane Goodall has influenced my life. I am still unable to describe what it feels like to call her a personal friend. She epitomizes the saying that "one person can make a difference."

Los Angeles science teacher JOHN ZAVALNEY discovered new directions and a new life through Roots & Shoots organizing.

JANE AS EXEMPLAR

Part of the difference between a teacher and an exemplar, or role model, is one of action and intent. A teacher teaches as an intentional act and recognizes who and what is being taught, while an exemplar teaches more intuitively, through example, and often through the image of a life well lived and powerfully expressed.

Jane has done many remarkable things in her life, and among the most obvious of those was to show, by example, that a woman could do something dangerous with style and grace. People were moved by that aspect of Jane's story. They were not moved in the same way as if they had taken a class or gone to the lectures of a brilliant professor and come home with an idea to think about. Very often, they were moved at a more fundamental level, through absorbing the meaning of a picture, an image, or a series of images. They saw Jane on television or in a film or displayed in glossy photographs inside the *National Geographic* magazine. Jane in her role as exemplar didn't affect people so much in the details or through analysis but rather by way of the image or story, and so the Jane Effect in this case operated through an intuitive grasp of who she was and what that meant. What people intuitively grasped was this. She was tough, but she was not a typical tough guy. Although she herself was once inspired by the fictional action figure Tarzan, she was not Tarzan. She was Jane, a woman of spirit who could out-Tarzan Tarzan but was also openly sensitive, expressed empathy and compassion, cared about her subjects in a traditionally feminine or maternal way. Jane was, in short, the kind of role model who always stayed female and feminine and yet casually shed the standard frills of traditional femininity to become more completely herself.

In the opening essay of this section, Smita Dharsi describes Jane's exemplar influence as having begun with a physical event. When Jane first arrived in Tanzania in 1960 to begin her chimpanzee research, she stopped first in the town of Kigoma to purchase supplies from Ramji Dharsi and give his new daughter a loving hug. Of course, Jane's influence continued far beyond those first inspired moments. In the second essay, primatologist Debra Durham writes of seeing a film of Jane in the seventh grade. She notes excitedly, "Jane didn't have a job like other grown-ups I knew, especially women." The idea kindled by that first image grew, and over time it expanded with other images and ideas from Jane's example. Anthropologist Lynne A. Isbell was moved by the image of Jane, in this case a photograph on the cover of her book *In the Shadow of Man*, to learn more about this woman who lived dangerously and well. The exemplary Jane led Isbell to change the course of her life by discovering what it means to be engaged passionately with the world.

Of course, being moved to action by Jane's example did not mean there was a specific map to follow or job to do. Not everyone can study primates in the wild, after all. But a more fundamental part of the exemplary image had to do with a certain empathetic and compassionate way with animals—the kind of relationship most children understand but then, in growing up, often forget. So it's not surprising that the exemplary Jane would reach people early, and, as with Katharina Jakob and Stephanie Feldstein, move them in new directions. Helen Forster writes of being a shy child who loved all animals and understood, through her own experience with kittens, that animals could have emotions, personalities, awareness, and presence. She then saw, in a magazine, pictures of a young woman living among wild chimpanzees who was as beautiful as a movie star and "incredibly brave" and dedicated to her animals.

Jo-Anne McArthur writes very specifically about Jane's impact as an image, one of "a woman in khaki pants and white shirt . . . working to her heart's content for animals and the environment amidst the lush backdrop of the African forests." McArthur describes herself as having studied Jane and thus she works, following Jane's example, to be "a messenger for animals."

As one of the Stanford University undergraduates who came out to Gombe, Nancy Merrick's early dream of studying chimpanzees in Africa with Jane Goodall came true. That dream led to her career as a family physician and an author, but she eventually returned to Jane and Gombe where she discovered "There is no higher calling than being a champion for those who lack voices." For Sonya P. Hill, the dream began when she was eighteen months old and her parents first took her to a zoo, where she was "completely hypnotized by the apes." When she was eight, she noticed that Jane Goodall was doing everything that she herself had wanted to do. Debra Merskin found her hero in the fifth grade upon watching a film about Jane Goodall who illustrated that one could make a difference in animals' lives. That childhood vision led her to the University of Oregon where she teaches "the disconnect between how animals are represented and their lived experiences." Kate Kitchenham, meanwhile, credits Jane Goodall as "the first and probably the most important" example she had growing up.

For Debra Teachout, Jane "blazed the trails" for women who wanted to work with animals. And she guided Teachout, a veterinarian, into understanding "animals as individuals each with their own personality and desires." Jane's move from scientist to activist also resonated with Teachout, who began to advocate and educate on behalf of all animals. Jane Miller's childhood discovery of Jane Goodall led not to chimpanzees or Africa but ultimately to a career in psychotherapy, with her two golden retrievers becoming co-therapists and "an integral part of [her] clients' healing processes." This led Miller to found

Healing Companions, which teaches shelter dogs to become psychiatric service dogs. For Zoe Weil, president of the Institute for Humane Education, Jane was a childhood role model who inspired her to become a "humane educator." Polly Thurston's youthful discovery that she wanted to study animals like Jane led at first to a college major in ecology and animal behavior, early work as a wildlife biologist, and later careers as an environmental educator.

For Jessica Pierce, the attraction of Jane's example came from knowing that "Jane loved the animals she studied, and that her way of being with them, quietly and respectfully observing their lives, was good." Pierce went on to study religion and bioethics before returning, finally, to animals. Meanwhile, Denise L. Herzing discovered an interest in animal minds and developed a passion for studying dolphins. Jane was for her the role model who showed it was possible to "embed oneself into the social world of another species." And Hope Ferdowsian describes Jane as having "stepped up and quietly led the way forward," enabling others to address professionally the psychological reality of animals, and sometimes, as in Ferdowsian's case, to study scientifically what happens when that psychological reality has been damaged.

I've so far described Jane's exemplar effect as something that touches women, particularly when they're young and still exploring themselves and their world. But it is easy to imagine that boys and young men might also find that image and story compelling. Daniel R. Tardona writes of a transformative moment he experienced in the neighborhood medical clinic, coming across pictures of Jane and her apes in the National Geographic magazine, opening up "a whole new world of animals and wild places." Shubhobroto Ghosh describes how an image of Jane struck him early on and included "the mystique and aura of the woman who redefined man." Later he met her in person, and she provided the moral model of the person he wanted to be. Tripp York, formerly a college professor teaching religious studies, was moved by the image of Jane because she lives her life "passionately—as if it were a gift." And so, as he writes, he cofounded Dominion, a sanctuary for farm animals.

Finally, Andrew C. Currie, an advocate for endangered wildlife, suggests that embracing Jane as a role model can positively transform boys, who so often learn to suppress their empathetic side. Jane showed him that "it is OK to listen to [his] heart, to care about animals and speak for their well-being," even when—make that *especially* when—you're a boy "growing up in a macho culture of hunting every critter."

—D. P.

Being Held by Jane

SMITA DHARSI

In the deep recesses of my brain lies a faint memory of being held by Jane. I was just a few months old when she and her mother, Vanne, first arrived in the small and remote Tanzanian town of Kigoma, at the edge of Lake Tanganyika. Jane was about to embark on a most remarkable expedition to a wild place, Gombe, about a two-hour boat ride from town. This is where she studied the wild chimpanzees by living among them in the forest. It was 1960, a time when it was yet unimaginable for any young woman to take on such an extraordinary assignment, but the presence of her wise mother somehow made it acceptable. My father, Jamnadas Ramji Dharsi, and my grandfather ran a store and petrol station in town. Jane must have needed supplies, and I expect my father invited her and her mother to come in from the store and into our house for lunch or perhaps dinner cooked by my mother—or at least a bracing cup of chai—since my parents always welcomed friends, old and new, that way.

I like to imagine that Jane's embrace that day sparked certain special neurons in my brain and awakened my soul to the beauty of nature. But Jane also had a slower and probably deeper effect on me during the years that followed our first introduction to each other. Jane, Vanne, and soon many others involved in the chimpanzee research began stopping to buy supplies, to have a meal or a cup of chai, to stay overnight when necessary, or to fill up on petrol my father trucked out to the Kigoma airstrip. So I saw her many times, and I admired her in the way a small child admires a special grown-up who seems to be a hero.

And I was filled with the stories my father told about Jane and her research. Relayed in the evenings under the stars, they stirred me with awe and excitement. Like water falling on the desert floor, the stories were giddily absorbed, and I grew up with visions of a magic land filled with wondrous creatures. I personified trees, felt their emotions. Gave names to rocks and shells. And all living beings—insects, birds, reptiles, mammals—became my childhood friends. During the day, I would escape to my own expeditions into the wild, overgrown area behind the house and, following Jane's example, write down my observations in a notebook.

When I was six or seven years old, my father brought home a copy of *In the Shadow of Man* and explained the story and its significance with infectious exuberance. Since English was my third language, I stumbled over the words without much comprehension, but the pictures, combined with the stories my father told and my own childhood experiences, made the book intensely fascinating. It was one of the few books in the house, and I leafed through the pages again and again, as if studying for a hard course in college. So my childhood was an idyllic life, and I was full of dreams about what I was going to do when I grew up, how I would connect with nature and animals just like Jane did.

All this came to an abrupt end one day in 1971 when the government decided to nationalize our store in Kigoma. The family had to leave Kigoma and go to the big city of Dar es Salaam. From there I was sent to England, a strange and alien place, and I went through adolescence there with little emotional or financial support. My father continued to communicate with me about Jane's research and whereabouts, though, and sustaining me through that hard time were the visions and memories I had of Gombe and the natural world.

I eventually came to New York City, where I struggled to get through college in order to become a teacher. Then one day my father came to visit, and he brought two tickets to a lecture by Jane Goodall at the Museum of Natural History. I went and was mesmerized: Jane's message, her imagery, the words, and her kindness spoke to my soul once again. Later on, in 1991, my father sent me a letter and brochure announcing the birth of Roots & Shoots. I was fortunate to be a teacher by then and thus to find myself in the company of two dozen young children who were thirsty for nature. I introduced them to Roots & Shoots, while animals, trees, rocks, insects, and all the rest of the natural world became the basic elements of my classroom project designs. Today, I am able to go home to Kigoma and to Gombe every year and help the Roots & Shoots community there, which returns me to the pleasures of a childhood I once thought I had lost.

So thank you, Jane, for sparking on that day in 1960 those certain neurons in my brain and then again for showing me, by your example and through the images and stories you created, what it means to stay whole and connected to animals, nature, and the human community.

SMITA DHARSI, born in Kigoma, Tanzania, has been an educator in the United States for the last twenty-five years. She has been creating Roots &

Shoots projects with her students since 1991. She is forming a nonprofit organization to support Roots & Shoots projects in Tanzania.

Start + Heart

DEBRA DURHAM

As a seventh grader growing up in a small town, I watched Jane Goodall in *The Wild Baboons of Gombe* in social studies with keen eyes. Jane didn't have a job like other grown-ups I knew, especially women. Watching animals in the wild? How amazing (though the term du jour was *awesome*). I wrote the assigned summary and added that I wanted to live vicariously through Jane Goodall's work. What a perfect chance to use *vicarious*, a new vocab word from English class. But sadly the phrase also reflected the fact that, while I was intrigued and inspired by the Goodall story, I didn't yet realize I could become a primatologist myself one day.

Years later, I started university as a communications major. In the time since learning about Gombe, I'd been thoroughly put off by my science classes, even though I loved animals and was curious about nature. Science sometimes made me feel bad because I was forced to dissect animals—a worm, a crayfish, a frog, and a pickled piglet. Those experiences make me cringe to this day. I begged my lab partners to do some of the cutting, but even watching and acting as scribe was horrible. Knowing that a cat dissection was part of the following term, I decided to stop taking biology. I didn't return to science until an elective anthropology class reconnected me with Jane's work. I learned about her studies of chimpanzees using tools, having culture, experiencing emotions; but most important for me were the stories about the lives of individual chimpanzees she studied and cared about so much. Jane showed me that science didn't have to be distant and detached. Seeing Jane use both her formidable brain and her generous heart to ask questions and effect change was a big part of what inspired me to reconsider my career and eventually make scientific research on behalf of animals my profession and my life's passion.

As a primatologist, I draw from Jane's stories over and over again for inspiration and dedication. I love that whether testifying before Congress or talking with schoolchildren, she links knowledge and action. Pushback or harsh words about animal advocacy? Jane Goodall has handled them gracefully, so I can too. Skeptics objected when Jane used terms like *tool* and *culture* when referring to the lives of chimps, so why should I be bothered if people raise eyebrows when I describe primates experiencing depression or PTSD? Not everyone got on board right away when Jane started talking about jealousy or grief with her study subjects, but over time, her research and the ways she spoke and wrote about chimpanzees sparked significant shifts in how science and society think about animals. I try to model her perseverance in hopes that I too can raise people's awareness and empathy toward animals. I'm also grateful for her studies because they have directly affected my own research. My colleagues and I have been able to draw from her findings on emotions, ask new questions about chimpanzees' psychological lives, and seek ways to put all of the evidence to use for the animals.

DEBRA DURHAM is an ethologist whose work explores the psychology and welfare of chimpanzees and other animals. She is also a cofounder of CAMP for chimps, recently launched in Uganda.

She Led Me to Passion

LYNNE A. ISBELL

Before I learned about Jane, I wanted to be a veterinarian because I thought that's what people who love animals do, and when I entered college I started on that path. During an internship with a local veterinarian, however, it became clear that that profession was not right for me. When I asked the vet why he became one and he replied, "It frees me up to play golf three times a week," I was taken aback. I was looking for passion in my work. I wanted a calling, not just a job that would allow me to do what I really wanted to do. I also had a couple of very light-headed moments around blood, which I erroneously attributed at the time to skipping breakfast. When that happened, I had to go outside for some fresh air, and that's how I realized I also wanted to work outside.

Then, out of the blue, Jane appeared. As I browsed my university's bookstore I discovered *In the Shadow of Man*, and on the cover I saw a young woman who looked not unlike me walking behind two chimpanzees and surrounded by green forest. At that moment, my life changed. If she hadn't written her book, if I hadn't gone in the bookstore, if someone hadn't ordered her book to sell there, who would I be today? Most certainly, not the person I became. The cover image so appealed to me that I immediately grabbed the book and bought it. And when I read Jane's words, my eyes were opened. She revealed to me that someone could actually make a living by observing animals, by being outside, and by learning about people of other cultures—all experiences I valued highly. They were my trifecta, and my path was clear from then on.

My college encouraged new ideas, and I was able to develop an individualized program of studies. I majored in ethology, the science of animal behavior, and I soon had numerous opportunities to hone my observational skills. These included an internship to observe the behavior of bongos, sable antelope, and Indian rhinos at the National Zoo. For my senior project I was able to watch semi-free-ranging desert bighorn sheep. After college, I volunteered to observe the behavior of bonnet and rhesus macaques at the primate center of the University of California, Davis, and that led to a paying job to observe the behavior of domestic cats at the veterinary school.

While I watched cats, UC Davis instituted a new graduate program in animal behavior. Although I hadn't planned to get an advanced degree, this was too good to pass up, so I applied. Alas, I was rejected . . . but not disheartened. Soon came the opportunity to study red colobus monkeys in the Kibale Forest of Uganda for two years. That was better than graduate school. Finally, I was living my dream. When I returned to California, I reapplied to the Animal Behavior Graduate Group and was accepted. But by then, I had been bitten by the Africa bug, and when I had the chance to go back for my doctoral research, I jumped—this time to Kenya, where I study primate behavior and ecology.

In Kenya I once had the chance to meet the real Jane. I saw her in a car one day, as she waited for her host—a rare chance to talk alone with her. Torn between wanting to share with her how she influenced my life and letting her wait in peace, I'm embarrassed to admit that I was insensitive. But I didn't know if I'd have another chance. I hoped she'd view what I was saying as a compliment, not a bother, but in my uncertainty, I talked much too quickly and inarticulately. I'm pleased to have another chance now. This time, I hope, Jane will be able to absorb my gratitude in her own good time, because the words will always be there.

So Jane, I give you a simple and heartfelt thank-you for showing me the path to ethology. I have indeed been blessed with a life full of passion for studying animal behavior, especially in the wilds of East Africa.

LYNNE A. ISBELL is a professor of anthropology at the University of California, Davis, with an interest in primate socioecology. She has done fieldwork in Uganda and Kenya, as well as in Madagascar, Tanzania, Rwanda, and the Democratic Republic of the Congo.

Look Closely

KATHARINA JAKOB

I never met her. Even when she gave a lecture in a nearby city, I never succeeded in meeting her because the tickets were sold out within four or five hours. Nevertheless, Jane Goodall has been part of my life since I was a child. I first heard about her in the early seventies. My father told me about this young woman who had turned her back on civilization to start a completely different life in the wild African jungle studying chimpanzees. Holding my breath, I hung on my father's words—"jungle," "chimpanzees," and "brave young woman" being among them.

For my father, it was just a bedtime story. For his seven-year-old daughter, it was a first glance at future possibilities. Like a window that suddenly swung open. If someone like Jane Goodall could go into the jungle, so could I.

"I guess Dian Fossey, Biruté Galdikas, and I have been role models for many other women," Jane Goodall once said in an interview. She was absolutely right. She inspired me to go out in my own private jungle—our garden and the copse not far from my parents' home, the shores of a lake nearby—observing every animal I could discover. There were swans and ducks, blindworms and squirrels, sparrows and blackbirds. Sometimes my mother found me kneeling in front of a frog. She talked to me, but I didn't hear anything. The whole world was focused on this little animal who jumped away when my mother moved.

Jane slipped out of sight for me when I was in my twenties, a time when I was figuring out how to lead my life. She returned with the first dog who entered my home and changed it from the very beginning. I had grown up with dogs, but this dog was the first I chose. More precisely, he chose me. "It's just a dog," people would say when I tried to explain his unique character. But Jane would whisper in my ear: "Look at this personality!" I read about her dog Rusty, who taught her that animals have an emotional life similar to ours. This scruffy, wild, and merry creature who decided to share his life with another species was the best link I knew between the animal kingdom and the world of humans. So I changed my profession from actress to journalist. Supported by my inner Jane Goodall and with help from my dog, I started to write about animals.

The most important thing Jane Goodall taught me is to doubt the common notion that dogs need our leadership. Do they really? Maybe they need our respect more than anything else. When Jane went to the African jungle, she knew only that she didn't know anything. So she was forced to look closely. This was her chance to find out what no one knew then: that chimpanzees use tools. It was a discovery so fundamental, so pioneering, that humans have had to change their outlook on animals and on themselves.

KATHARINA JAKOB is a German journalist and author living outside Hamburg with her husband and their dog. She is interested above all in the relationship between humans and animals.

Growing Up Jane

STEPHANIE FELDSTEIN

When I was six years old, I assumed that every girl wanted to be Jane Goodall. A respected scientist who got to hang out with chimpanzees, she was proof that a woman could do anything. We often grow out of our childhood heroes. We come to realize they're flawed, only human. Or entirely fictional. Leaving them behind is part of growing up. But I grew into Jane Goodall.

It didn't happen right away, or even intentionally. I didn't map out my life to follow in her footsteps as a primatologist any more than I took the path my parents had sketched out for me to become a veterinarian.

I'd always instinctively understood that to love animals meant treating them well. In high school, I started to explore the ethical questions raised by how our society uses other species. I inevitably rediscovered Jane Goodall. Unlike other scientists, Dr. Goodall never shied away from recognizing animals as individuals or expressing our responsibility to nature. As I prepared to head for college, her words reminded me what I'd first learned when I was six: I didn't have to let labels and conventions define me.

I started working in animal rescue during college. After graduation, I worked for an environmental organization. I knew I was in the right field, but I hadn't quite found my niche. Then I fell into organizing, through a job that started as editing an animal welfare blog and morphed into leading online campaigns to protect animals and the environment. Suddenly, my love of animals became bigger than me, with articles and actions reaching people around the world.

The experience of your words being read and shared is both exhilarating and intimidating. You find like-minded people, but you also open yourself to criticism from complete strangers. Especially, it seems, when speaking out for animals. Around this time, Dr. Goodall appeared on *The Daily Show*. She spoke of facing criticism with compassion, about hope and the future. She re-energized me to become a better activist. The fact that she was graceful and funny while doing it only reinforced her heroic status in my mind.

I recently stepped into a new career, a turn in the trail to focus on wildlife conservation and the impacts of human population growth and overconsumption on the survival of other species. Population can be one of the most challenging issues to talk about. Yet in my first days on the job, there was the influence of Dr. Goodall, a leader in the movement, once again showing me the way like my own personal spirit animal.

I've come a long way as an activist and an adult. Still, I want to be Jane Goodall when I grow up. Not in the sense I had when I was six. Now I want to inspire, to be inspired, and to change the world. Though I wouldn't object to hanging out with chimpanzees.

STEPHANIE FELDSTEIN is the population and sustainability director at the Center for Biological Diversity. She previously worked at Change.org and has more than fifteen years of experience in animal rescue and advocacy.

My Childhood Hero

HELEN FORSTER

When I was a young girl I was terribly shy, and I didn't socialize comfortably with other children because of this. However, I had a vivid imagination and felt a deep affinity with animals. I especially loved cats. Still do. I like to say I've had cats in my life since I was in the womb. I've never been without a cat (and I've treasured every one) for more than a few months.

One of my earliest recollections is of observing the birth of kittens. Our long-haired cat Snowball had so many litters she'd gotten the nickname Mother Cat from my mother. The cats we had in our family were my trusted and beloved friends. I held regular conversations with them, recognized each of their personalities and quirks, and knew and loved each cat's particular emotional makeup. In fact, I loved all animals. As a youngster I briefly dreamed of becoming a veterinarian, though I soon realized my true calling was to be an actor and musician.

But perhaps you can imagine the impact it had on me when, as a young child in the early '60s, I learned about a young British woman who'd gone to Africa to live with chimpanzees. I read an article and saw photographs of Jane Goodall in Africa interacting with the chimps and was absolutely mesmerized. Jane was movie-star beautiful, for one thing (impressive to me as a young girl, I confess); and she seemed incredibly brave to do what she was doing. And all on the behalf of animals! She instantly became my hero. I read everything I could about her, collected photos, told everyone I knew about her work. My admiration continued into my adult years, and I love to follow her efforts even now.

Forty years later, Jane appeared on *eTown*, the National Public Radio program I cohost. I was so excited at the prospect of meeting my hero I could hardly sit still that day. When the appointed time came for her to arrive, all of us at the theater felt the excitement in the air. Suddenly, the door opened and there she was—still beautiful, with a kind, gracious, almost regal presence. At some point our production manager walked me over to meet her. Well, of all things, that old childhood shyness suddenly overtook me, and I froze. I managed to stammer out a hello and not much more. It was a terribly awkward moment. But Jane never let on that anything was amiss. She took the time to talk with me and put me at ease. In time, thank goodness, I relaxed, and we had a lovely conversation, one of several that have taken place since that day.

HELEN FORSTER is a professional musician and actress. Since 1991 she has appeared each week on *eTown*, a popular music/variety radio show aired around the world.

If You Can Do It, I Can Do It Too

JO-ANNE McARTHUR

Dear Dr. Jane,

I don't remember the exact publication or film that introduced me to you when I was a young girl, but I remember the impression and the idea with which I was left. It was an image of a woman in khaki pants and white shirt and a simple ponytail, a woman working to her heart's content for animals and the environment amid the lush backdrop of the African forests. This is the way I'll always think of you, though I've since met and photographed you many times now, and always in cities on vast stages or classrooms or behind a podium.

Your image isn't two-dimensional—you are an icon, an idea, and an ideal. (Sorry to objectify you like this, Dr. Jane, but it's true!) I'm thankful that you've put yourself out there, allowed yourself to be swept along this path, allowed people to be inspired by you. You accepted this mission, one that was bigger than you—a mission to which you've dedicated your life.

When I learned of you as a girl and started following your work, your life, and your mission, I knew something: I am like you.

Am I really bold enough to write that?

I was a young girl, and I saw in your life my own future, the sort of life that I had no doubt I would lead as well, one of independence, passion, sacrifice, and deep joy in the work. I didn't know what that work was going to be until my early twenties, when I became a photographer. Later I became an animal rights photographer, eventually traveling to all seven continents to document our all-too-often tragic relationship with animals worldwide.

Over the years I've attended many of your talks, and I will admit that I've studied you and how you navigate this world. I've continued to learn and be inspired by how you deliver a message, how you focus on kindness, all the while carrying within you a great tragedy, which is the full knowledge of how we humans use and abuse our world and our animal kin. You seem to me at once a rock, a wise woman, and the bearer of an enormous responsibility. It must be, at times, isolating for you. The irony is that you continue to live one of the most exciting, dynamic, and important lives of our time, and you are surrounded by people who love and admire you.

I aim to be a messenger for animals, and I work hard to do this, while also trying to be a person of hope and inspiration for others. I want people to understand the gravity of what is happening to our animal kin, and I hope that my work urges others to change, move, and act the way your work urged me to change, move, and act. You've shown me that a life of adventure, beauty, and great responsibility is possible. I've told many people over the years that I am what I am and I do what I do, in great part, due to your inspiration and influence. I'm deeply grateful for your work, and I'm deeply grateful for the choices and sacrifices you've made along your journey.

JO-ANNE MCARTHUR is the photographer and author of *We Animals*, a subject of the film *The Ghosts in Our Machine*, and a long-term volunteer with the Jane Goodall Institute.

All My Life I Wanted to Be Jane Goodall

NANCY MERRICK

Let's just say it. All my life I have wanted to be Jane Goodall. As soon as I saw that first National Geographic film, it was my dream to study chimpanzees in Africa with her. So imagine my unbelievable good luck at age nineteen to have the chance to actually do it! Ever since, my life has followed hers in one way or another.

There was Gombe, the Stanford Outdoor Primate Facility, Jane's Human Bio class, and then the awful days of the 1975 kidnapping. After that, our lives reconnected in Washington, DC. Jane, knowing my concerns for captive chimps, included me in a meeting to address how the USDA could better ensure the psychological well-being of captive chimpanzees. Later, my young family and I jumped into her Roots & Shoots program, launching an elementary school group that would stay intact even after those same kids headed off to college. Their lives were changed in wonderful ways, and they went on to work in the Peace Corps, public health, and conservation—and to be citizens of the world.

My favorite Jane story comes from 2008. I had taken my husband and young-adult children to Gombe to see the place that so changed my life. We arrived to find Jane there and were invited to her home on the beach. Instantly, we noticed she was nursing her shoulder, and when we asked why, she spoke of following a chimp up a steep hillside and falling back down it as the more-than-hundred-pound rock she had reached to grab hold of gave way. She somehow managed to keep the rock from crushing her and landed, bruised and battered, at the bottom. Nevertheless, she reassured us, she was doing fine and still able to use her shoulder. Being a physician, I offered to examine her, but she'd have none of it.

"Jane," I finally told her, as sternly as possible, "if we were in the United States, I would put you in the car and drive you to the orthopedist right now."

Without missing a beat, she retorted, "Thankfully for me, we're not in the United States."

I had met my match, and though I worried intensely about her, I could not get her to budge. A week later, we learned that Jane's shoulder not only had a small fracture but was dislocated as well. How did she do it? I've never seen anyone tolerate a dislocated shoulder for more than a few hours, let alone a week. And then it occurred to me: that was how much she did *not* want to leave Gombe. She knew that if I diagnosed the dislocation, it would mean leaving immediately. In that moment, I began to understand the sacrifice she has made by traveling more than 300 days a year on behalf of chimps and the planet. She has given up countless days at her beloved Gombe and what could have been an easier and more fulfilling life.

And so, what I have learned from Jane is this: being a world-class warrior requires untold passion and sacrifice—and there is no higher calling than being a champion for those who lack voices.

NANCY MERRICK is a primary care doctor practicing family medicine and internal medicine. She is the creator of ChimpSaver.org and author of *Among Chimpanzees: Field Notes from the Race to Save Our Endangered Relatives.*

Following Jane

SONYA P. HILL

When I was around eighteen months old, my parents took me to a zoo in Bristol, UK. At the zoo, my parents noticed that I had become completely hypnotized by the apes. Spellbound. They recognized that something magical was happening for me in that moment, and from that moment on, I would tell everybody that I was going to work with "monkeys" one day.

My lovely parents supported my new passion by buying me children's books about primates and encouraging me to find out everything I could about them. Then, when I was eight years old, I watched a National Geographic rerun about the Gombe chimpanzees on Sunday evening telly. Suddenly, here was a lady doing everything I had felt in my heart I wanted to do but didn't even know was possible!

A few weeks later, my sister spotted a secondhand copy of Jane's *In the Shadow of Man* book at an antiques fair that we had been dragged to by our parents, and with relish I spent my pocket money on it. I read it avidly and wanted to be part of this amazing woman's world one day. And so, in my early teens, I wrote a letter to Jane that was probably full of things like *I want to be just like you when I grow up.* And she wrote back.

It was a beautiful, handwritten letter, full of warmth and encouragement to follow my dreams. It felt like receiving a letter from a long-lost aunt. And so I did follow my dreams. Having kept in touch with Jane, I went on to set up the first Roots & Shoots group in the UK in 1992, and I organized fundraising events for JGI and the Dian Fossey Gorilla Fund while at senior school. I represented JGI at events for youth in Stuttgart, Germany, and at the United Nations in New York. I studied anthropology at university, and I overcame a full-on needle phobia so I could take my jabs and set off for Tanzania to work on R&S with Jane, where I fulfilled my childhood dream of seeing the Gombe chimps with her. (I was hospitalized with falciparum malaria just after leaving the forest—but, hey, I'd seen the Gombe chimps!) I visited Gombe with her again in 1998 and went on to do a PhD in ethology, focusing on apes.

From there I joined Jane's work in Africa. Initially I was to be based at the Tchimpounga Sanctuary. Unfortunately, a civil war in the country broke out on the day of my flight there, and I moved into the study of zoo animal behavior and welfare back home. I went on to become the convenor of the Primate Society of Great Britain's Captive Care Working Party, and I organized the Society's Gombe 50 conference in the UK in 2010 to celebrate the amazing work that Jane pioneered. I am proud to be part of Jane's extended family.

SONYA P. HILL is an ethologist specializing in the behavior and welfare of captive wild animals, especially primates. She is a trustee of JGI UK.

Daytime Dreaming

DEBRA MERSKIN

I met my hero one afternoon in 1969. I was in fifth grade at Hart Elementary School in a tiny rural northern Michigan town. We fifth and sixth graders were rounded up and organized boy/girl/boy/girl and led into the put-ty-colored gymnasium for a movie. I do not remember what class it was for or why we were to see the film. I do know, however, that when the projector rolled, I met Jane Goodall and knew who I wanted to be when I grew up. Goodall was only twenty-six years old when she went to Tanzania's Gombe Stream Reserve and not much older than that when a photographer from *National Geographic* first captured her working with the animals.

To a skinny little towheaded girl like me, she represented possibility— the possibility of working with animals and making a difference in their lives. Ah, to study animals—to be permitted a peek into their world and to advocate for them as important individuals in the world. Such bliss! That film said to me that a girl could aspire to be someone interesting, exciting, and special.

In her work with the Gombe chimps, Jane Goodall demonstrated the power of compassion and connection, and she showed that this approach to study, through the perspective of care, could produce legitimate sci-ence. I now know that her early work was criticized and dismissed by some in the scientific community as amateurish (she didn't have a univer-sity degree yet) and that her narrative, qualitative approach was looked on with skepticism. Fortunately, that didn't stop her.

Growing up, I thought I would follow in Goodall's footsteps, not with chimps necessarily, but studying and advocating for creatures in the natu-ral world. But something happened along the way, and I lost sight of what most mattered to me. I ended up nowhere near those early goals of study-ing zoology, anthropology, and psychology. The closest I have come to it is to study the symbolic significance of "othered" beings as shown in mass media, in advertisements, in films, and on television programs. However, in the last few years, the obvious connection between the treatment of marginalized human beings and animals has pant-hooted for my attention. Rather than fearing rejection among traditional academic peers, I took my courage from Jane's example, that same "reason for hope" that inspired me as a child, to advocate for animals.

I now teach university courses that deal directly with the impact of the disconnect between how animals are represented and their lived experiences. Inspired by Jane's example, I encourage young journalists to change the language of the press, to describe an animal as a *him* or *her* rather than as an *it*, and I explain why that matters.

DEBRA MERSKIN, associate professor of journalism and communication at the University of Oregon, is a media studies scholar dedicated to revealing discrimination in all its forms, particularly the parallels between racism, sexism, and speciesism.

From Blackbirds and Flo to Dogs and Ruby

KATE KITCHENHAM

I must have been about eleven years old. I sat in the garden, daydreaming, enjoying nature, sun, and wind. Suddenly I realized that a blackbird was jumping just next to me across the grass. He held his head to the side, watching the ground to see if any earthworm would fall for his tricky replication of rain. He didn't take any notice of me, and I felt like I was in paradise. I sat there for an hour enjoying one bird after the other coming closer and closer, thinking I was a tree or something else unexciting. I felt part of a big something, and exactly from that moment I knew what I wanted to do: translate the world of animals to people. I wanted people to become infected with curiosity about the inner life of animals too, so that they would respect and want to save all those other beings.

This early passion has never changed. I had some helpers, even if they didn't know it or know me. Jane Goodall was the first and probably the most important one, because she accompanied me through all my decades. By the time I was thirteen, I'd read all of her and Konrad Lorenz's books. By then, my career plan had become more precise: I wanted to be a scientific journalist who writes about ethology. So I studied biology and focused on canid behavior and primatology. Today when I write books and articles about dogs and I talk to people about how to understand their companion animals' body language, I see in some faces a glow of sudden enthusiasm. When I imitate a dog's behavior, I see that people unexpectedly realize how close we all are in our feelings and intentions and that it is easy to be compassionate about other living beings, whether that other being is a dog, a gorilla, or a blackbird.

Jane has inspired me to work naturally and to do something every day. I loved the way she did her research in the era of behaviorism, how she rebelliously chose names for her chimps instead of numbers. I empathized with Flo and her children and was thrilled that Jane took Flo as an example for how to raise her own baby, Grub, in a time when other mothers put on clinical shirts before they fed their babies with sterilized bottles. When I had my first baby, Ruby, in 2000, I also tried to do what I had learned from Flo. It worked out fine. Today she is thirteen years old, and she wants to do something in her life.

KATE KITCHENHAM, author of five books about dogs, is a science journalist and an expert commentator on the German television show *Der Haustier-Check* ("The Pet Check").

Canada Geese and Undercover Videos

DEBRA TEACHOUT

How do you verbalize a thank-you to someone of international stature who has mentored you, supported you, inspired you, and, above all, given you hope without even meeting you?

I am about a generation younger than Jane Goodall, so while she blazed the trails, I followed them. I wasn't quite as adventuresome as Jane, but I became a veterinarian, focusing early in my career on the care of companion animals and urban wildlife. Her vision of animals as individuals, each with his or her own personality and desires, resonated deeply. I remember treating and rehabilitating four Canada Geese simultaneously for different maladies, and after working with them over the course of a few weeks, I began to marvel at their differences. One was shy and frightened, one bold and aggressive. One was curious and social, and one kept inventing tricks to play on us. Certainly we recognize the individuality of companion animals, and Jane described the various chimpanzee personalities, so why not Canada Geese?

Jane's career course adjustment in 1986 from scientist to advocate again blazed a trail that I followed. I remember reading about her career transformation during the Understanding Chimpanzees conference in Chicago and thinking that chimpanzees could have no better advocate. I did, however, wonder how she could trade contact with her beloved chimpanzees for the grueling job of endless educating, lobbying, and advocating. She would endure the heartbreaking and horrifying work of witnessing the abuse of chimpanzees in order to stop it. Yet she still has hope, and that lesson is also incredibly important to me.

About five years ago I attended an event comparable to Jane's life-changing Chicago conference of 1986, and I saw then that her decision made all the sense in the world. In fact, the conference I went to altered my focus almost overnight from the care of individual animals to the welfare of billions of animals, mostly those raised for food. I was subsequently asked to review footage from an undercover video showing the living conditions and treatment of egg-laying hens stuffed into dark, cramped battery cages for their entire short lives, and to offer my professional opinion concerning the welfare of the hens. The video was heartbreaking, but I could think of no better use of my veterinary degree than to try to help these unfortunate animals. Since 2009, I have offered opinions on about twenty undercover videos witnessing horrific animal living conditions, treatment, and abuse. I have advocated for respect for all animals and humane standards of care. When I encounter resistance and criticism or get discouraged that improvements aren't happening fast enough, I remember Jane. I draw energy from the decisions she made and her seemingly endless tenacity to make things better for animals.

Thank you, Jane. I envision a better world for animals because of you.

DEBRA TEACHOUT practices small-animal medicine in Chicago. She received the 2013 Veterinary Advocate of the Year Award from the Humane Society Veterinary Medical Association in recognition of her advocacy for the humane treatment of animals.

Jane Paved the Way for Healing Companions
JANE MILLER

I spent my early years devouring everything I could discover about Jane—her books, stories, and television programs. One day in fourth grade I arrived home from school and announced to my mother that I wanted to be Jane Goodall when I grew up. At that moment I had dedicated my life to vegetarianism and helping animals. But who knew that Jane would lead me on to discover my life's work and passion? Her wisdom, courage, and love of animals penetrated deeply into every moment of my life.

Through my childhood I nursed fledglings with eyedroppers, rode horses, adopted turtles left on the curbside, trained my dog, and became an advocate for Save Our Seals. In my first year of college, I immersed myself in animal behavior in an intensive research project. I studied the behavior of red kangaroos in captivity and explored ways that zoos could improve their facilities. When I turned fifty, I attended the British School of Falconry and learned hawk handling so that I could volunteer at the local raptor center, where I was committed to healing these birds so they could return to the wild. Such experiences set the stage for me to integrate my work as a holistic psychotherapist with the healing power of dogs.

My two golden retrievers became my co-therapists and are an integral part of my clients' therapeutic healing process. In the mid-'90s, I began devoting my time and energy to assessing clients for psychiatric service dogs, finding the appropriate shelter dogs, and training them to meet clients' specific needs. Jane's Roots & Shoots program provided the impetus for me to reach out to local organizations and collaborate with them to educate youth at risk, inmates at correctional facilities, and students about the healing power of the human-animal bond. My clients learn positive service-dog training techniques and stress reduction/relaxation techniques for humans and their animals, all of which provide them with greater self-confidence and self-worth.

Jane is my heroine and role model.

JANE MILLER, a clinical social worker interested in holistic healing, is the author of *Healing Companions: Ordinary Dogs and Their Extraordinary Power to Transform Lives*. She focuses on educating others to work with psychiatric service dogs.

In Jane's Footsteps

ZOE WEIL

Jane Goodall was a role model for me, as she has been for many girls. I wanted to be her when I grew up. I loved animals, and Jane offered a vision of how one could be with and learn from them. While I did not ultimately pursue ethology, I did work for a couple of months as a volunteer intern in a psychology laboratory at the University of Pennsylvania where chimpanzees were learning a symbolic language. Finally, I had the opportunity to work with chimpanzees!

Sadly, I quickly found that even the most seemingly benign lab research—teaching chimps to communicate in human language—could come with considerable ethical consequences. Due to potential aggression, Sarah, the most famous of Penn's language-using chimps, was caged alone and never allowed to interact with other chimps or with humans except through the bars of her cage. In fact, she had long ago stopped participating in the language acquisition work. She seemed bored, depressed, and angry. Caging the three-year-old chimps who had just begun their language work seemed wrong as well.

I stopped volunteering at the lab and became a full-time humane educator. I realized that I could help best by teaching young people about what was happening on our planet to animals, the environment, and people. This is what Jane now does every day. It looks like I followed in her footsteps after all.

ZOE WEIL, cofounder and president of the Institute for Humane Education, is the author of many books.

How Jane Influences My Life

POLLY THURSTON

When I was five years old, my father gave me a stuffed toy chimpanzee astronaut because I loved the astronaut chimp named Ham. Of course, at the time, I didn't understand real-life existence in the space program—how monkeys died in space and how Enos and Ham, the first chimpanzees in space, were really just babies like me, suffering what no baby should endure. I only knew that Ham was my spirit brother and that I wanted to be an astronaut like him.

A couple years later, Jane Goodall was featured in the *National Geographic* magazine. I begged my mother to read me her story and explain to me what this young woman was doing. To my amazement, I discovered that she was living in Africa very near a community of chimpanzees in order to study their behavior. She was photographed touching hands with and grooming chimpanzees. Right away, I realized that I wanted to be an animal observer like her.

In college, I studied ecology while exploring the behaviors of animals. After college, I worked as a wildlife biologist hooting for spotted owls in the Pacific Northwest. I also worked on environmental education projects, teaching ecological concepts through the arts (e.g., puppetry and storytelling) while focusing on animals as a theme. Many cultures have traditional stories with animals as the central figures. For me, Jane brings this love of animal stories to a modern-day reality. Jane influenced me as a young child to develop ideas about what was OK to feel and say about other species in a society that consistently devalues and discourages understanding the interconnection we have with all species. Her identifying chimps by names rather than numbers emboldened me to think out of the scientific box as well.

If as a girl I hadn't had a woman mentor who exemplified respect for all living creatures, then I doubt I would have linked my imagination to my love for other species. I may not have recognized the possibilities. Jane has shown us that ending war among ourselves will ultimately end our war on animals. Influenced by Roots & Shoots, I worked with a local elementary teacher to bring in the giant Peace Dove while joining ecology and poetry to teach about the Northwest's prairies.

Jane continues to inspire me to keep doing what I can do, no matter what. She gives me courage to keep trying in a world that continues to deny other species protection. Her example shows me a kind of love greater than the human construct, greater than species differences, greater than scientific curiosity, greater than ecological destruction—a love and respect for the wondrous diversity of this amazing planet.

POLLY THURSTON is an artist, poet, puppeteer, storyteller, environmental educator, wildlife biologist, caregiver, and gardener.

I Want to Be Jane Goodall

JESSICA PIERCE

When I was young, and people asked me what I wanted to do when I grew up, I had a ready response: "I want to be Jane Goodall." I loved animals and knew that I wanted to do something that brought me close to them. And from the time I was old enough to read on my own, I pored over everything I could find about Dr. Goodall, pondered the photographs of her with the chimpanzees, and imagined myself out there in the African forest too. Although I wouldn't have been able to formulate it at the time—nor would I have understood just how remarkable her approach was, given the usual ways people were studying animals—I knew that Jane loved the animals she studied and that her way of being with them, quietly and respectfully observing their lives, was good.

My mother encouraged my fascination. In fact, it was my mother who first introduced me to the world of Jane Goodall and supplied me with the books. Certainly, she did that for reasons beyond my love of animals. My mother is very astute, and she no doubt understood what a wonderful hero Jane Goodall would be for a young girl. Here was a woman who did not let people's prejudices about gender get in her way, who was a brilliant scientist, and who was brave enough to travel to Africa and tromp through the forest with wild animals by herself.

For a variety of reasons, I did not become a wildlife biologist or an ethologist. Instead, I followed my passion for religion and philosophy. After college, I entered seminary, got a doctorate in ethics, and pursued a career in bioethics. Over the past decade, my professional work has finally veered back into the terrain that I most love: animals. By a series of coincidences, I had the pleasure and honor, six or seven years back, of getting to know Jane's friend Marc Bekoff. Dr. Bekoff invited me to collaborate with him on a book project, and I found myself once again poring over Jane Goodall's work, this time for part of my research. When our book *Wild Justice: The Moral Lives of Animals* was about to be published, Marc asked Jane if she would write a testimonial for the book jacket, and she graciously agreed. I'm sure Dr. Goodall has no idea how meaningful that small paragraph is to me. It is far more than a mere book blurb.

Even though my work is worlds away from Dr. Goodall's and I never did manage to become a wildlife biologist, I realize that there are many paths to the same destination. I still aim to achieve some tiny measure of what Dr. Goodall has achieved: a greater understanding of our animal kin and, with this greater understanding, a larger measure of compassion and protection.

I still want to be Jane Goodall.

JESSICA PIERCE is a bioethicist, writer, and internationally recognized scholar in animal and environmental ethics. Her most recent book is *The Last Walk: Reflections on Our Pets at the Ends of Their Lives.*

From Gombe to the Bahamas

DENISE L. HERZING

As a young student in the 1970s, I felt a passion for trying to understand the minds of other animals. Dolphins especially fascinated me because of their large brains and highly social nature, and yet they were relatively unstudied in the wild. At that time, most of the research on dolphins was done in captivity, but I was determined to find a place in the wild where I could observe dolphins under water.

The work of Jane Goodall with chimpanzees, Dian Fossey with gorillas, and Cynthia Moss with elephants made it clear that it was possible to embed oneself in the social world of another species. So the barriers were broken, and I had those pioneering women as models for working long term and noninvasively with wild dolphins. In 1985, I finally located a place in the Bahamas where wild Atlantic spotted dolphins seemed to tolerate humans in the water. After exploring this possible field site, I concluded that it could be the ideal place for a long-term study. Of course, like any other field study, there were challenges: weather, access to the animals, and funding. But I had those three strong female models who had demonstrated that with dedication and perseverance I would gain an understanding of a wild social species. And by using the techniques of benign observation, respecting the social etiquette of the species, and setting an effective pace of interaction—all aspects of Jane Goodall's work with wild chimps—I succeeded.

Since 1985, I have spent four to five months each year observing wild dolphins under water and documenting their behavior, sounds, reproduction, relationships, and social habits. The year 2014 represents my thirtieth year with the same resident community of free-ranging Atlantic spotted dolphins in the Bahamas. I still enjoy being out in the field where I can freely squeak like a dolphin and frolic in the waves, although I doubt my dolphin imitations are as good as Jane's chimpanzee sounds. But like Jane, I have watched the generations of my study group pass by, so that I can now look forward to witnessing a fourth generation of dolphins and can anticipate all the benefits that understanding another sentient species might bring to our planet.

DENISE L. HERZING is the founder and research director of the Wild Dolphin Project, a study of Atlantic spotted dolphins in the Bahamas.

The Graceful Trailblazer with a Message of Hope

HOPE FERDOWSIAN

Jane Goodall's graceful courage blazed a trail for many of us. Her example has spoken volumes, particularly to women working on behalf of vulnerable individuals. As a physician who cares deeply about the suffering of animals—human and nonhuman alike—I have taken note of the ways in which Jane conducted her work.

At a time when men dominated her field, she stepped up and quietly led the way forward. She bravely assigned names, personalities, and relationships to individuals who until then were largely invisible as sentient beings. She wrote and spoke unapologetically about the cognition, emotions, and predicaments of nonhuman animals. Jane's early research also set the stage for a study my colleagues and I conducted, which demonstrated that chimpanzees can suffer posttraumatic stress disorder (PTSD), depression, and other psychiatric disorders. Jane established that chimpanzees have rich and complex lives and emotional bonds similar to those of humans. Years later, my colleagues and I studied how devastating the disruption of these bonds can be.

In 2011, we published our findings showing that chimpanzees with prior histories of captivity and laboratory experimentation were more likely than chimps living in the wild to show signs of mood and anxiety disorders. In our study, we tried to understand more fully the nature and epidemiology of psychiatric conditions among great apes that are comparable to human psychiatric disorders. We used a combination of approaches: psychiatric, ethological, and veterinary. In the first phase of the study, we determined that behavioral signs of mood and anxiety disorders were more reliable than established human psychiatric diagnostic criteria, when applied to published case reports of traumatized chimpanzees. In the second phase of our study, we applied the behavioral diagnostic criteria to data collected on chimpanzees living in sanctuaries as a result of previous use in laboratory research, illegal trade and seizure, or being orphaned. Chimpanzees who had been transferred from laboratories to sanctuaries in our study had been exposed to various degrees and periods of confinement, removal from social groups, invasive procedures, induced diseases, or chronic isolation. A small sample of the wild chimpanzees had documented histories of injuries resulting from snares, spears, or comparable physical trauma. We found that 58 percent of 168 chimpanzees living in sanctuaries met the standard psychiatric criteria for depression, compared with 3 percent of 196 chimpanzees in the wild. We also noted that 44 percent of chimpanzees in sanctuaries met the standard criteria for PTSD, compared with 0.5 percent of chimpanzees in the wild.

The mental anguish of the chimpanzees of our study resembles that of human survivors of torture and other forms of violence. Editors at *Scientific American* recognized our study's ethical implications and cited our research findings in their call to ban invasive chimpanzee research in the United States. Fortunately, the resilience of many of the chimpanzees we studied also resembles the resilience of my patients. Despite their traumatic histories, chimpanzees in sanctuaries are now able to experience joy, safety, and love—largely as a result of the heroic work of sanctuary staff, who have also been influenced by Jane's work. Her message of hope and peace lives on.

HOPE FERDOWSIAN is a physician in both internal medicine and preventive medicine, and she is a public health specialist at George Washington and Georgetown Universities.

From Inner-City Kid to National Park Ranger

DANIEL R. TARDONA

Almost every day, as I don my park ranger badge and place my flat hat upon my head before going out to the park, I have a fleeting thought. Seeing the tall trees and thick undergrowth as I walk to the park museum and visitor center, I imagine primates swinging from tree to tree or a chimpanzee mother calling to her children. This might seem strange coming from a fellow who grew up in an inner-city slum, very far from any of the beautiful national parks where I have worked during the past twenty-six years. So allow me to explain.

I was born and raised in Brooklyn, New York, in a poor neighborhood. My only encounters with wildlife, other than roaches and rats, were with the pigeons perching on my second-floor tenement window or the stray dogs and cats who sometimes roamed the streets below. While I was extremely curious about those beings with whom I shared my inner-city young life, my awakening occurred one day when my mother took me to the neighborhood medical clinic. I was sitting at the clinic, nervously waiting to hear my name, when mother—maybe she was trying to get me to sit still for once—passed over a clinic's copy of the *National Geographic*. Aware of my interest in animals, she told to me to look through the pages to find pictures of animals.

It was August of 1963, and I was nearing my tenth birthday. Inside that magazine were pictures of this young lady with her hair in a ponytail living among chimpanzees in the African jungle. It is difficult to put into words the excitement I felt, as a whole new world of animals and wild places suddenly burst into my awareness. That was the spark. It was the beginning of my desire to study science and to acquire some understanding of animal behavior that, although I didn't know it then, would lead me down many other exciting paths. Something about those pictures and the words Jane had written caused me to want answers about if and how animals think and feel about their world. Being a good Catholic schoolboy, I also had deeper questions about animal souls. I wanted to know how animals and humans were alike and how they were different. That was phase one of Jane's influence on my life.

As time went on, I began to follow her work, and through that I became more aware of the threats to all animals and the environments supporting them. I gained a greater understanding of our commonality with animals and our role as stewards over their lives and the places where they live.

My journey has been a convoluted one, much too complicated to describe completely here, but Jane led me all the way. My job as a National Park ranger now is to help people discover their own intellectual and emotional connections with the meanings inherent in the natural world and the animals who live in it. My life goal is to help people relate to and care about the welfare of animals and the natural world. I thank Jane for my awakening in pursuit of a rich life's work and for my continuing evolution from naturalist and scientist to conservationist to activist—and so much more.

DANIEL R. TARDONA has been a National Park Service ranger for more than twenty-five years, with stints at Cape Hatteras Seashore, Gateway Recreation Area, and Great Smoky Mountains Park. He lives in a ranger house with his wife and a very large housecat named Shiloh.

Follow Your Heart

SHUBHOBROTO GHOSH

Images have multiple meanings. They can convey emotions, dreams, aspirations, individuals, and hopes. Like millions of others, I had an image of Dame Jane Goodall that had first come to me via television and the *National Geographic* when I was a student. Later on, films, television serials, books, and the Internet added to the mystique and aura of the "woman who redefined man." As an individual who brought compassion into the realm of hard science, she had already attained a saintly status when I had the opportunity to spend two days with her in person in Kolkata.

I was working as a journalist for the *Telegraph* newspaper in Kolkata when on January 19, 2007, I received a telephone call from a colleague at the British Council urging me to attend a press conference that was scheduled with Jane Goodall in an hour's time. The occasion was the beginning of a two-day personal association with her that led to two exclusive interviews as well as a chance to accompany her to the zoo and attend her public lecture at Nandan, a famous theater in Kolkata.

Dame Jane has had a profound influence on everything I have done, in my journalism, and in my work with captive zoo animals. The motto of the Jane Goodall Institute—*Every individual matters. Every individual has a role to play. Every individual makes a difference*—is intrinsic to my outlook on life. Jane Goodall has made me realize that one has to be sensitive to individual differences among animals and people, and one should never lose sight of the fact that many animals share the same feelings of love, joy, sadness, anger, and pain that we do. These values and principles have been applied throughout my work with captive zoo animals in India and abroad. I have always tried to share an animal's feeling in captivity while watching him or her inside a cage. Thanks to Jane Goodall, I am more sensitive to the plight of single animals in captivity, especially Polo, the lone gorilla in Mysore Zoo, and Shankar, the single African elephant in Delhi Zoo. Given that every individual counts and that gorillas and elephants are both social animals, their captivity merits all the attention we can garner for wild animals in captivity anywhere.

Dame Jane Goodall was a guiding force for me in the Indian Zoo Inquiry investigation, and she is a sensitive writer whose autobiography *Reason for Hope* is one I avidly imbibed. Her principle of moral evolution greatly influenced me. I have now written a book based on my life's experiences checking zoos in India and England that explores many philosophical issues I consider important for conservation and animal rights, including the issue of keeping great apes and other animals in captivity. Dame Jane has honored me by generously writing a foreword to my book. I could not have asked for a better or more distinguished endorsement.

So thank you, dear Jane, for all your work in the field and for encouraging me to follow my heart and giving me reason for hope.

SHUBHOBROTO GHOSH is a former journalist for the *Telegraph* whose work has also appeared in the *Times* of India, the *New York Times*, the *Statesman*, *Asian Age*, and the *Hindu*. Ghosh is a senior programs officer at TRAFFIC India, an international network that monitors wildlife trade.

From Professor to Scooper of Poop
TRIPP YORK

Many times, as I was heaving large chunks of elephant poop into a wheelbarrow, I would ask myself, Just how did I go from being an assistant professor of religious studies to cleaner of elephant dung?

It all started when I was asked to teach a seminar called Living Lives That Matter. Despite being the least qualified person on campus to teach the course, I jumped at the opportunity. My incredibly bright students and I worked through a variety of complex questions: What does a meaningful life look like? What does work have to do with what it means to be human? What do religion, love, death, politics, family, faith, and friendship have to do with living a life that matters? As you can well imagine, it was the kind of course that needed to be longer than one semester.

We spent the majority of our time reading as many books as I could conceivably fit into one semester. We examined biographies, essays, novels, short stories, and plays. Actually, the main problem with the course was that all we did was read. In retrospect, a little less reading and a little more *doing* would have been helpful.

At the last minute, I included a section on wildlife conservation. Initially, this struck a number of my students as odd. After all, when it comes to life's big questions, doesn't it make more sense to read Aristotle and Shakespeare? Why bother reading Annie Dillard's take on weasels or learning why Clem Coetsee stressed the importance of dehorning rhinos? Indeed, when surrounded by the safe concrete walls of the university (where the only nature students typically encounter is in a biology lab), such readings did seem to be a stretch.

As we started to examine the saints of the wildlife conservation movement, such as Helen Freeman, Dian Fossey, Lawrence Anthony, and Jane Goodall, students started gravitating toward the vision these conservationists shared. This process was due not to any verbal arguments made by these activists; rather, their vision was compelling because of the tangibility of their lives. What these conservationists did, what they contributed to the world, and how they lived were so utterly concrete. Whether it was Fossey's fight for the gorillas, Anthony's relationships with elephants, Freeman's unparalleled work with snow leopards, or Goodall's work with chimps, my students were moved by their ability to live life passionately—as if it were a gift. My students were not, however, the only ones to be moved.

Inspired by the work of these conservationists and not sure where to begin, I began serving as a keeper's aide in a zoo. While this was indeed a valuable learning experience, it wasn't enough. My wife (who is completing her PhD in ecological science) and I are now in the process of creating an animal sanctuary for abused and neglected farm animals. Following the reference in Genesis 1:26, we are naming it Dominion. Our understanding of *dominion* is that it is about the proper care for all of creation. Our intention is not to argue that point, but to show it. For such inspiration, we have the Jane Goodalls of this world to blame. They are, after all, the reason I went from professor to scooper of poop.

TRIPP YORK, a visiting assistant professor of religious studies at Virginia Wesleyan College in Norfolk, is the author or editor of ten books.

The True North on My Compass
ANDREW C. CURRIE

Jane Goodall has been my hero since I watched her on TV as a kid in my living room in Mississippi. She showed me that it was OK to listen to my heart, to care about animals, and to speak up for their well-being. This was no small feat, growing up in a macho culture of hunting every critter. Jane was the only person who gave me this point of view.

Later, when I was in my forties, I became a successful software entre-preneur, sold my company, and had time and money to do good in the world. How exciting! I felt at my core I wanted to help nature and wild-life. Jane was one of the leaders I aspired to be. Her message of hope, her encouragement to take action, and her insistence that one person can change the world, as expressed in her book *Reason for Hope*, had a huge impact on my thinking at this time.

Partly because of seeing Jane on TV as a kid, I started taking eco-tours in 2001, along with my wife, Diane, and two close friends. We went to several countries in Africa to see what was going on with endangered wildlife, including chimps and gorillas. I visited mountain gorillas and chimpanzees in Uganda, watched lowland gorillas and looked for chimps in the remote forests of Gabon, experienced the vast migration in the Serengeti, was moved by being in the presence of elephants in South Africa, and was awed by the sheer beauty of nature expressed in Botswana. The book *Eating Apes*, by Dale Peterson, which was recommended with a testimonial by Jane on the front cover, really opened my eyes and fired me up. I wanted to do everything I could to make life better for my fellow nonhumans, especially the great apes and other endangered wildlife. Jane inspired me to act boldly when I saw her speak in Denver at the Jackson Wildlife Film Festival and at the Wildlife Conservation Network Expo.

Jane is *the* role model I look to. She is the one who helps power every-thing I do as an advocate and philanthropist for endangered wildlife. The groups I have helped to launch and grow (such as LoveAnimals.org), the prairie land and wildlife I have helped to protect in my adopted home state of Colorado, the grants I make to help wolves, mountain gorillas, ele-phants, cheetahs, and people living alongside endangered wildlife are just a few examples of Jane's *direct* influence on my life, values, and approach.

Thank you, Dr. Jane Goodall, for who you are and all you do! You are a wonderful, powerful spirit who has improved our world forever. I love you.

ANDREW C. CURRIE is a software and Internet entrepreneur, investor, advocate, and philanthropist, passionate about increasing empathy and funding to help endangered wildlife.

JANE AS VISIONARY

A visionary is someone who sees further than most people, someone who is advanced in her thinking, ahead of her time, and she is often that way without trying to be. A visionary is someone who, like Jane, recognizes certain things to be true even when a boisterous crowd of contemporaries, including the anointed experts and authorities, say differently. Jane's particular vision involves a new way of seeing animals and the human connection with them, a more direct and, indeed, a more scientific way—that is, a more logically Darwinian way—even though some of the powerful knights and lords of science in her younger days disagreed and sometimes dismissed her work as amateurish and unscientific.

Yes, she made those early discoveries. She was a great pioneer, and her pioneering work went far beyond advancing scientific knowledge. By doing such a small thing as identifying her study subjects by name rather than assigning them numbers—as sociologist Leslie Irvine recalls in the opening essay of this section—Jane began to change a scientific habit. And by insisting from the start that the animals she studied were not the complex machines of reflex and instinct so handily imagined by American behaviorists and European ethologists, she helped change the paradigm. To her way of thinking and representing, according to her *vision* of the world, the animals she studied were fundamentally actors in their own drama.

Jane's role as a visionary might first be appreciated as a piece of cultural history—which is how Carol J. Adams, author of the second essay, represents the Jane Effect as it appeared at Yale University in 1972. It was a time,

Adams writes, when people flocked in like disciples in order to listen, and they thought of themselves as being "part of something radically important breaking through into ordinary consciousness." Dale Jamieson develops that theme and more specifically describes Jane's approach as an important part of the "cognitive revolution that would eventually enable us to see intelligence and sentience widely distributed in nature." Angelique Richardson, considering perhaps a broader sweep of historical time, suggests that Jane's act of personalizing animals should be compared to Charles Darwin's revolutionary argument that humans and other animals are all part of the biotic continuum.

Other contributors point out that this new way of seeing animals represents a profoundly important psychological shift. Philip Tedeschi declares that Jane's story of her one-time interaction with David Greybeard, a cross-species exchange of invitations, brought him to the study of human-animal associations. William Crain speaks of Jane's work as having inspired his own sense of animals' "spiritual emotions, which are outside the bounds of mainstream biology and psychology." Celia Deane Drummond elaborates on the topic, noting that "other creatures are . . . also able to sense and respond to energies that theologians recognize as being divine." And in his wonderful essay "The Awareness of Souls," Stewart J. Hudson implies that the psychological and spiritual dimensions of Jane's vision are indistinguishable and that this fundamental "awareness of souls," human and nonhuman, "reminds us that there is a connection among all creatures, great and small."

Vivek Menon describes the visionary Jane as someone who can "touch the lives of people without meeting them." That indirect touch brought Menon to change careers, so the Jane Effect was transformative at a personal and practical level; but the change was also, ultimately, an ethical one. Yes, seeing the connection among all living things and knowing that nonhuman animals live in much the same experiential world as the human animal brings us almost inevitably to think in moral terms and then to act. In this way, Jane's effect on others can be characterized as one of "becoming-witness," to recall the evocative expression introduced by Deborah Bird Rose.

Many of us have always intuitively understood the ethical implications of Jane's vision, and her work with chimpanzees has helped make sense of and give voice to that intuition. Jonathan Balcombe places Jane's vision in the context of a historic and "global struggle for justice for all sentient creatures." But as Balcombe goes on to say, it is not merely the message that has had such a powerful effect—it is also the messenger. Philippa Brakes writes of her childhood responses to seeing casual cruelty to animals in a Thailand wildlife park. Years later, she read the "thoughtful, quietly revolutionary work" of Jane and others and better understood the rich, deep nature of the animals she was trying to protect. And finally, Natalie Houghton speaks memorably of the world she grew up in, where children were taught to suppress their natural empathy and sense of injustice when witnessing cruelty to animals. Jane's work taught her that the suppression itself was wrong and that her own intuitive childhood reaction was the more moral one. And Jane's Roots & Shoots program showed her that she was not alone. Houghton concludes, "I feel blessed to be a part of this growing movement of people who want a humane, peaceful, and sustainable world."

—D. P.

Even a Small Thing

LESLIE IRVINE

Dear Jane,

When students ask me what they can do for animals, I say that even small things matter. I tell them how you gave the chimpanzees names, rather than numbers. Now I have the chance to thank you not only for naming them, but for so much more.

Let us raise a collective pant-hoot to rejoice at how you recognized that chimpanzees think and feel, and another collective pant-hoot to thank you for defending that idea. Thank you for finding the strength and the persistence to do that.

And I'll add yet another thank-you for working so tirelessly for peace when so many have forgotten that we are all connected—and for reminding us that we need Roots & Shoots, and that together, we can make a difference.

But even a small thing, like giving a chimpanzee a name rather than a number, can change the world.

LESLIE IRVINE teaches sociology at the University of Colorado, Boulder. Her research focuses on human-animal interaction. Her latest book, *My Dog Always Eats First*, examines homeless people's relationships with companion animals.

A Gift Given

CAROL J. ADAMS

During the autumn of my first year at Yale Divinity School, 1972, a remarkable thing happened at the downtown campus. Jane Goodall came to give four lectures in the large auditorium of the law school. After the first lecture, which included a film of chimpanzees, word spread. Arriving forty-five minutes before the second lecture was to begin, a *New York Times* reporter who came there to interview Jane barely found a seat. Even though I was living up the hill at the divinity school campus, I felt the air change. The reporter captured the electric feel on the campus:

The next day it was even more crowded, the aisles choked with students and faculty members who were sitting on the floor, the high window ledges of Sterling Law auditorium crammed with latecomers who had scaled the walls and come in from the outside. At the fourth and final lecture "Chimpanzee and Human Behavior: Some Similarities and Differences" the situation was a fire marshal's nightmare: every inch of space downstairs and in the balcony was occupied, doorways and window ledges were jammed and scores of people were turned away.

It is rare when we know at the time that we are witnessing something radically important breaking into ordinary consciousness. But I could feel it happening that week. Everyone talked about it; everyone said they had heard her (a statistical impossibility). Forty years ago, it felt that Jane Goodall's work of challenging the divide between *us* and *them* broke those circles wide open, and all of Yale wanted to hear her speak.

CAROL J. ADAMS is the author of *The Sexual Politics of Meat* and many other books and the coeditor, with Lori Gruen, of *Ecofeminism: Feminist Intersections with Animals and the Earth.*

Jane Goodall, the Beatles, and Me

DALE JAMIESON

As a child of the 1960s, almost everything that changed my life seemed to have an English accent. I remember the first time I heard the Beatles as a high school student in Oakland. Their music rocked my world, especially the harmonies on "I Want to Hold Your Haaaaand." I already loved rock and roll and rhythm and blues, but hearing it with an English accent through the hormones and sensibility of four lovable moptops from working-class Liverpool seemed dangerously different. I had always talked back to my teachers, but now I was cheeky rather than insubordinate, a young surrealist rather than a sullen adolescent.

I was also prepared for Jane and her accent. I grew up near the ocean with animals; loved my dog, who was smarter than most of my friends; and was an antiwar activist and environmentalist. In college I studied philosophy and religion, and in graduate school I specialized in philosophy of language. My dissertation supervisor, Paul Ziff, had the incredibly unfashionable view that the term *language* really stands for "human linguistic behavior," and the study of *that* was obviously a branch of ethology. He threw some books by Konrad Lorenz and Niko Tinbergen my way and drove off in his Porsche to play tennis.

By then, tales of Gombe were widely circulated, but in the rarified world of philosophy of language, Chomsky ruled, and even we dissidents were more interested in Washoe than Greybeard. This was not all bad: we were working our way through a cognitive revolution that would eventually enable us to see intelligence and sentience as widely distributed in nature. At the time, though, it was not easy to see where Jane's vision of chimpanzees fit into that much more lab-bound, theoretical narrative. Her stories were the stuff of the *National Geographic*, not the *Philosophical Review*.

Marc Bekoff helped me to see Jane's work against a broader background. Ethology was not just Lorenz and Tinbergen but an even larger and more wonderful undertaking that at its best was as risk-taking as John

Lennon's "Number 9." This was a liberating insight. The influence of this new view of animals was growing on me. And when I learned about Jane's battle with the scientific establishment over naming animals, I began to see that not only was she a boundary-breaking ethologist, but that she was also one of us. She cared about all animals—not only chimpanzees—and she cared about them as individuals, not just as members of a species.

Things then moved rapidly. Jane and I were both among the original signers of the 1993 Declaration on Great Apes, which sought their inclusion in the "community of equals" and the recognition of their rights to life, liberty, and protection from torture. In 2001, finally, I met Jane in Boston, and in 2002, she wrote an endorsement for my book, *Morality's Progress*. Increasingly I saw her not only as an ethologist and animal advocate but also as a gift to the ages. I introduced Jane at a lecture in 2013 as a visionary who has her arms around the whole world—animals, people, the future, and the entire planet.

DALE JAMIESON is a professor of environmental studies and philosophy, an affiliate professor of law, and director of the Animal Studies Initiative at New York University.

Darwin, Goodall, and the Scientific Imagination

ANGELIQUE RICHARDSON

When Jane Goodall gave animals minds, names, and personal pronouns, she was in good company. A year after Queen Victoria ascended the throne, Charles Darwin declared, "He who understands the baboon

would do more towards metaphysics than Locke." Biology, or, more precisely, the study of animals, could contribute more to our knowledge of
the world and the nature of being than philosophy. As this short sentence
moves from the specificity of the baboon to the heights of Lockean philosophy, the figure of the baboon is dignified, reoriented in the cosmos,
and the Cartesian tradition in philosophy of mind is upturned. Two centuries earlier, Descartes had declared animals automata: "Although many
animals show more skill than we do in some of their actions . . . it shows
rather that they have no intelligence at all, and that it is nature which acts
in them according to the disposition of their organs." By contrast, Darwin
and Goodall were enthralled by the intelligence and subjectivities of the
animals they studied, refusing detachment, implicitly calling into question the merits of objectivity if that meant disallowing respect, sympathy,
and empathy for their subjects.

Darwin loved dogs. He wrote, "I can believe almost anything about
them." His fox terrier Polly and his retriever Bob (the dog with the hot-
house face) feature in his *Expression of the Emotions in Man and Animals*
(1872), a work that bustles with detail about the mental and physical lives
of animals, from affectionate monkeys, yawning baboons, fighting deer,
impatient horses, curious deer, excited rattlesnakes, moving to the anthro-
pomorphic—dogs have ennui, just as Darwin remarks that all animals
"feel Wonder." Mammals jostle with humans—frowning babies, playing children—and all are fully integrated into the naturalistic economy
of emotion. In the year that it was published, Darwin told the women's
suffrage campaigner and anti-vivisection activist Frances Power Cobbe
that he had come to believe dogs have a conscience. A century later, Jane
Goodall began her career as, in her own words, "somebody loving nature
and animals."

Chimpanzees have an important part to play in *The Descent of Man*, particularly when Darwin stresses continuity: "The ears of the chimpanzee and orang are curiously like those of man, and I am assured by the keepers in the Zoological Gardens that these animals never move or erect them; so that they are in an equally rudimentary condition, as far as function is concerned, as in man." And, referring to orangs and chimpanzees as "the animals which come next to [man] in the series," Darwin suggested, through quietly effective understatement, that both had similar wants and powers of reasoning. Even when discussing instincts, which he considered progressively common down the animal hierarchy, he still dignified animals by referring to them as "he" and "she"—something Jane Goodall, in defiance of conventional scientific practice, would be taken to task for just over a century later. Goodall's first article, in *Nature* (1964), on her work with the chimpanzees in Gombe, was returned with "he" and "she" replaced throughout by "it." She reinstated her own pronouns, and this time they made it past the scientific censors. She considered that a small victory, as indeed it was. The article, focused on tool-using and aimed throwing, treats the chimpanzees as individuals, revealing them to be resourceful, playful, careful, at other times fearful, and, on occasion, when faced with encroaching baboons, seeking to intimidate.

Jane Goodall's discoveries take forward Darwin's own observations. Following several visits to the orangutan Jenny in London Zoo (he was allowed inside her cage), Darwin recorded in his C notebook: "Let man visit Ouran-outang in domestication, hear expressive whine, see its intelligence when spoken [to], as if it understood every word said—see its affection to those it knows,—see its passion & rage, sulkiness & very extreme of despair; . . . and then let him dare to boast of his proud preeminence."

In *Descent* Darwin observed: "It has often been said that no animal uses any tool; but the chimpanzee in a state of nature cracks a native fruit, somewhat like a walnut, with a stone." He continued, "In the Zoological Gardens a monkey which had weak teeth used to break open nuts with a stone; and I was assured by the keepers that this animal, after using the stone, hid it in the straw, and would not let any other monkey touch it. Here, then, we have the idea of property; but this idea is common to every dog with a bone, and to most or all birds with their nests."

Goodall's article in *Nature* revealed that chimpanzees were not only using but making tools. The renowned anthropologist Louis Leakey cabled his response: "Now we must redefine 'tool,' redefine 'man,' or accept chimpanzees as human." And just as Goodall's dignifying of chimpanzees was met with censorship and resistance, so the press resisted or derided Darwin, with the *Times* insisting on "an absolute difference in kind" between humans and animals. Yet others were more welcoming, with the *Lancet* praising Darwin's theory of common descent and approving the anthropomorphism: "Dogs and the higher monkeys he thinks undoubtedly express pleasure by grinning and incipient smiles; chuckling and a kind of laughter can be induced in chimpanzees and young orangs by tickling or presentation of favourite food." Although people still commonly think of anthropomorphism as universally bad, an embarrassing act of irrationality, in fact a judicious anthropomorphism is essential for accessing and understanding animal subjectivity, as Jane Goodall first began to show us more than half a century ago.

Darwin's work was embraced by writers and artists, just as, today, new correspondences between art and science are developing, perhaps most notably in the growth of the interdisciplinary field of animal studies. "So the world gets on step by step towards brave clearness and honesty!" declared George Eliot to her feminist friend Barbara Bodichon. Nonetheless, in her early work Eliot held on to human distinction. In *The Mill on the Floss*, which appeared a year after Darwin's *Origin*, a young Maggie Tulliver is already "gifted with that superior power of misery which distinguishes the human being, and places him at a proud distance from the most melancholy chimpanzee." But in her last novel, *Daniel Deronda* (1876), for which she took notes from Darwin's *Expression*, there was a new emphasis on animal kinship, as Darwin's emphasis on human-animal continuity led to a new questioning of boundaries between body and mind, emotion and intellect, passion and reason.

Like Charles Darwin in his century, Jane Goodall in hers has seen things with the curiosity of the poet who makes things strange and new, insisting on the humanity of animals. It is an unspeakable tragedy that as our understanding of nature increases, so does the human destruction of the planet. But the Jane Goodall Institute, dedicated to education and conservation, sets out Goodall's reasons for hope. They lie in the human ability to solve problems, change and take responsibility, the triumph of the human spirit, the resilience of nature, and the determination of young people.

As Darwin was able to see cooperation and mutual aid throughout nature, so Goodall has become a United Nations Messenger of Peace, her vision of hope developed from the close, careful, and undetached observation of the lives of animals.

ANGELIQUE RICHARDSON is an associate professor of English at the University of Exeter. She has published widely on nineteenth-century science, literature, and culture and has additional research interests in animal studies.

Waking Up with a Smile

PHILIP TEDESCHI

I often wake up with a smile. Every day I am thankful for the work I get to do at the Institute for Human-Animal Connection here at the University of Denver. I am the executive director of this institute, which was created to promote greater understanding of the complex relationships between humans and nonhumans.

I have had the opportunity to orient my compass toward kindness and the humane treatment of people and animals over the last thirty years, but it has not come without doubts and controversy regarding the seriousness of this as a life's work. I've had to defend my passion on many occasions, both professionally and personally, and advocate for myself in order to study human-animal interactions. The research done by Jane Goodall has been of immense importance for me in choosing to chart this course. Of course, her new approach to studying animals was significant, but for me, in those first years of my career and to this day nearly thirty years later, it was her description of how the chimpanzee David Greybeard extended his invitation to her that I found so compelling.

Jane's work had major implications for science, the study of animals and humans, and the field of ethology. It forced us to redefine *human* and *animal*. It shifted the paradigm. But for me it was that single interaction between David Greybeard and Jane that allowed me to see the importance of studying human-animal interactions and relationships.

My days have been filled with an appreciation for such important anecdotes, and I have come to recognize the plural of anecdote is data. Although I have never been to Gombe, I was fortunate to discover the trail defined and established there. Jane Goodall's early work allowed me to recognize that in careful observation and reverence for the relationships we have with the living world around us, we will find our own most reliable purpose and identity. My journey has unfolded in almost every possible dimension of the human-animal connection, and I have encountered it in all its ungainly contradictions, its callousness, and its senseless cruelty but also its never-ending and inspiring beauty. I don't regret a single day.

PHILIP TEDESCHI is a clinical professor and the executive director of the Institute for Human-Animal Connection at the University of Denver's Graduate School of Social Work.

The Value of Fresh and Open Observation
WILLIAM CRAIN

In *Reason for Hope*, Jane Goodall said she was glad that she began her research on chimpanzees prior to graduate training. An unschooled observer, she gave the chimps names and paid attention to their individual personalities and emotions. If, instead, she had first attended graduate school, she would have been taught that science must be impersonal and that she must consider the animals only as numbers. Unrestrained by the research orthodoxy, she learned a tremendous amount about chimpanzees' emotional behavior.

   Goodall's account strengthened my sense that the best observation is often uncluttered by theory and scientific convention. In my developmental psychology writings, I have often called attention to Abraham Maslow's conclusion that the most creative people have a childlike capacity to see the world freshly and openly. Especially in the early phases of their projects, they try to perceive the world just as it is, in all its richness, without forcing their perceptions into predetermined categories. Jane Goodall has consistently exemplified this approach.

I have been told that other ethologists value a similar approach in their initial observations, but this is not always evident in their technical writings. To me, it's Goodall who most clearly illustrates the value of rich, open, and unfiltered observation.

Such observation became especially important to me in 2008, when my wife, Ellen Crain, and I founded a farm animal sanctuary. Our principal goal was to give rescued animals a loving home, but the farm also offered me an opportunity to learn firsthand about animal behavior. I wanted to learn about animals from their own perspective, and I also hoped the animals' emotional behavior would cast some light on the emotions of human children. I decided to spend my first years on the farm following Goodall's example. So I avoided reading experts' treatises on the farm animals and instead maintained a degree of naïveté—to simply see what the animals revealed to me.

Some of my animal observations may indeed provide insights into children's emotions. For example, when we first rescued goats, sheep, and other animals, they were often terrified and were silent for days or even weeks. This observation might provide psychologists with clues about the otherwise mystifying silence in children. Perhaps the children's silence is in response to an intense fear like that of our animals.

My most surprising observations have to do with spiritual emotions, which are outside the bounds of mainstream biology and psychology. Goodall, open to the full range of animal emotion, was struck by the possibility that chimpanzees experience a kind of spiritual awe at a waterfall. I have been more impressed by animals' states of deep peacefulness— states that seem to be similar to those of children in natural settings. But whatever form spiritual experiences may take, Goodall was once again among the first to show that our observations can extend beyond the current scientific orthodoxy.

WILLIAM CRAIN is a professor of psychology at City College of New York and cofounder of Safe Haven Farm Sanctuary in lower Dutchess County, New York.

Wonder and the Religious Sense in Chimpanzees
CELIA DEANE DRUMMOND

As a theologian, I have found the most thrilling aspect of Jane Goodall's insights in her account of chimpanzees contemplating a waterfall:

> I can't help feeling that this waterfall display or dance is perhaps triggered by the feelings of awe or wonder that we feel. The chimpanzee's brain is so like ours; they have emotions that are clearly similar, too, or the same that we call happiness, sadness, fear and despair and so forth; incredible intellectual abilities that we used to think were unique to us. So why would they not also have feelings of some kind of spirituality, which is really being amazed at things outside yourself. And it's the same with the start of the heavy rain. . . . Maybe it's defying the elements. . . . I think the chimpanzees are as spiritual as we are. But they can't analyze it, they can't talk about it. They can't describe what they feel. You get the feeling that it's all locked up inside them. And the only way they can express it is through this fantastic rhythmic dance.

This to me is mind-blowing. I believe that Jane is much closer to the mark than some evolutionary psychologists who track the evolution of religious belief through some kind of agent detection device in the brain that then eventually develops into a belief in an unseen God. Jane is sensitive enough and open-minded enough as an observer to consider that the waterfall experience is a marker of a genuine religious experience and not simply a transferral of capacities in response to a threat, such as snake avoidance. Of course, it is difficult to come to the firm conclusion that the wonder experienced by chimpanzees is in a direct evolutionary relationship with the wonder that human beings experience; but either way, there seems to be a convergence of a capacity for wonder in our nearest primate cousins.

Traditionally, theologians and philosophers have worked hard to render human beings exclusive in relation to other creaturely kinds and, by implication, superior to them. Jane shatters that portrait. It has not always been so, however. Hagiographic accounts of the earliest Christian saints regularly spoke of how other animals were responsive to God, often through the ministry of the saint who was prepared to spend time and pay close attention to them. Celtic Saint Cuthbert (634–687), for example, spent hours during the night in prayer submerged up to his neck in the sea. He perceived otters as agents responding to his needs and through his prayers, and on a journey, an eagle brought him fish. Later, as a hermit living on the island of Farne, Cuthbert described ravens showing signs of remorse after eating his crops. These creatures were equally servants of God, he thought, as he was.

Now, as Jane indicates, it is unlikely that these animals had any self-conscious awareness of what they were doing. But an inclusive understanding of these creatures in spiritual terms is a prominent aspect of the very earliest traditions of Christianity. Later scholars such as Saint Albert

(d. 1280), recognized emotions in other animals. The post-Enlightenment view of the world has shorn us from a deeper appreciation of the lives of other animals. Jane is correct—only humans can theologize, but that does not mean other creatures are not also able to sense and respond to energies that theologians recognize as being divine.

CELIA DEANE DRUMMOND is a professor of theology with a concurrent appointment in the College of Science at the University of Notre Dame.

The Awareness of Souls

STEWART J. HUDSON

During the time I was privileged to work with her, Jane was an educator who taught me more about the souls of animals (including us humans) than I could ever have imagined. The lessons she shared with me have remained and only deepened over the years.

What is the soul of an animal? It is what I see when I look into the beautiful brown eyes of my dog, Oliver. It is the gaze of the blue jays who adorn my front porch. It is the vision of a fisher cat wandering through the woods behind my house, casting the furtive glances of both predator and prey. Our mindfulness of the souls of animals creates a communication and an understanding that transcends language. This communication, well beyond forms that are the peculiar province of humankind, reminds us there is a connection among all creatures, great and small.

Why is this connection important? As Jane has shown the world, it induces empathy and understanding—traits that lead us to be more humane not only in our interactions with wild and domesticated animals but also with the natural resources and ecosystems that are part of the environment we inhabit. The awareness of souls also binds us, one to another, in a timeless way. I know that Oliver's soul will be with me always, and hopefully mine with his for all time. That connection brings comfort.

Jane has also taught me and the world that the wisdom associated with this soul connection opens us up to a new world of scientific inquiry and understanding. For if all animals have souls, then we are similar, so that what we learn about other animals has standing and can teach us more about ourselves. Rather than the historical hierarchies projected onto the animal kingdom that bias us toward judgment and preclude us from learning, we can accept that social behavior among other primates, whatever its nature, might be a window into how we behave (and how we might wish to behave).

The souls of animals bind us, one to another. Our mindfulness of the souls of animals provides timeless connections. These connections make humans more humane. They comfort us. They teach us. These important lessons Jane has given to the world for decades. She has shown us the way, for which millions of people, such as myself, and countless animals are forever grateful.

Thank you, Jane!

That is a good prompt for me to now stop writing and speak to my best friend, Oliver, in ways that transcend speech and time.

STEWART J. HUDSON, executive director of Audubon Connecticut and vice president of the National Audubon Society, was formerly executive director of the Jane Goodall Institute USA.

A Sage for Animals

VIVEK MENON

Ten years ago when I finally met her, I deduced that there is something of an Eastern sage in Jane Goodall. However, she first came into my life nearly thirty years ago, on a hot summer night in Delhi early in my first year at college. I was enrolled in chemistry by my father, an automobile engineer who ran a factory that made industrial paints and hot melts.

He must have thought I was destined to take over his business. He had not discussed this plan with me at any length, or I would have told him that my heart was set on zoology. If he had seen my room in the duplex flat where we lived, he might have had some inkling of my tendencies, as I kept assorted birds, turtles, and a monkey or two there, at various times. But he was too busy a man, preoccupied with his work, and in those days, bonding with sons was not an established fashion. In the same vein, telling your father what you wanted to do in life was not normal either. Thus, our first real conversation happened after I had spent a few miserable months studying chemistry and then was asked by my teacher why I was moping around and faring badly at college. I told him I wanted out. "Tell your father," he said.

He might as well have told me to bring the twelve-headed Hydra chained to my ankle. I asked him to do the deed. And so it was that my father, enlightened about my love for animals and my desire to study zoology, and despite his own lack of interest in the natural world, tossed me three dog-eared books one morning at breakfast. The first was E. P. Gee's *Wildlife of India*. The second was Iain Douglas-Hamilton's *Among the Elephants*. And the third was Jane Van Lawick-Goodall's *In the Shadow of Man*. It was a small Fontana paperback with black-and-white photographs. The one I remember was of a young chimpanzee lifting up the shirt of an attractive young blonde—Jane—with the caption, "We sometimes hid bananas under our shirts!"

I was totally hooked by the books, particularly Jane's, and I started my deviation from a career in industry and business to one as a zoologist and conservationist in the shadow of Jane Goodall. Much later, after I founded the Wildlife Trust of India, I met her and invited her to give a lecture in Delhi. Then in quick succession, I had the good fortune of being with her in Ireland, in the United States, in Holland, and then in Italy. Each time, I heard her passionately hoot like the chimps and saw her carry her old beloved stuffed monkey doll up the stage and hold various audiences spellbound by her passion. Each time, I turned to think about what she had done to me even without meeting me, and I knew the power she had to transform lives.

In Italy, in the shadow of some magnificent rosebushes and grape trellises, I spoke with her one evening at length about our work. She confided that she traveled over 300 days a year for animals. I told her that I only traveled 200 days and felt tired. She reached out and held my hands in hers. "But you must continue doing what you are doing, Vivek," she said, "for the animals, for the animals." Indeed, it is for the animals that we do what we do, but it is also for our own souls. And the quietude and inner strength that Jane Goodall has managed to spread to the animal protection world makes me think of her as a true sage for animals.

VIVEK MENON is executive director and CEO of the Wildlife Trust of India and advisor to the president of the International Fund for Animal Welfare. He is also a best-selling author and an internationally renowned conservationist with a passion for elephants.

Becoming-Witness

DEBORAH BIRD ROSE

Jane Goodall's life of witness is exemplary. The meaning of *becoming-witness* includes both attention to others and expression of that experience: to stand as witness and actively to bear witness. The stories Goodall has brought to the world are not comforting. Indeed, they tell us more about contemporary life than we would have wanted to know. As Goodall's life has been changed, so readers' lives are changed too. I am one such reader, and I write with immense gratitude.

Jane reconfigured science into an arena of witnessing. As a primatologist and ethologist she became a participant/observer, and so she gained an understanding that is the bedrock of becoming-witness. The lives and deaths of others really matter. They matter to each individual, and they matter to the group, which leads directly to the further understanding that others too inhabit worlds of meaning.

Becoming-witness to the chimpanzees' world of meaning brought into moral focus the cruelty and violation involved in killing them and in capturing and selling them for scientific research and other forms of consumption. The fact of human predation called for another layer of witnessing: activism and advocacy. One of my favorite books is *Visions of Caliban*, coauthored by Dale Peterson and Jane Goodall. Many of the stories are horrific, but the purpose of the book is not strictly to convey horror but rather to awaken conscience.

The knowledge that chimpanzees inhabit worlds of meaning is never far from sight. The suffering they endure when they are locked up in cages in animal experimentation facilities has an effect not only of immediate physical deprivation, but also of the loss of the world that had given their lives meaning. Dr. Goodall's account of a chimp named JoJo, kept in a metal cage in a laboratory, articulates the contrast between the world of meaning in which he was raised and the impoverished world he was forced to endure. She asks: "Did he sometimes dream of the great trees with breeze rustling through the canopy, the birds singing, the comfort of his mother's arms?" And she recounts the beautiful moment when JoJo reached through the bars to make contact with her. He groomed her wrist, and she looked into his eyes and spoke to him. Overcome with a complex set of emotions, she wept. JoJo reached out and touched her tears.

This is the most gripping layer of becoming-witness. Jane Goodall allows us to witness others who are witnessing us. Her brief story opens an interspecies dimension of mutual becoming-witness. This encounter, of course, rests on JoJo's capacity for becoming-witness even from behind the bars where "there is nothing to look at, nothing to play with . . . where family and friends are torn apart and where sociable beings are locked away . . . into solitary confinement." It takes place across a set of ontological iron bars as well, across histories of violence and cruelty, and across the largely one-sided story of human harm to animals.

Yes, becoming-witness takes us into tough places and shows us our complicity. But this is as it should be. All is not well in the house of life, and until we are able to achieve some sort of peace, as Jane Goodall's life shows us, we have a fourfold duty: to pay attention to others, to bear witness, to work for betterment, and to refuse to lose hope.

DEBORAH BIRD ROSE, a professor of ecological humanities at the University of New South Wales, is the author of numerous books, including *Wild Dog Dreaming, Country of the Heart*, and the prize-winning *Dingo Makes Us Human*.

Animal Biographer and World Changer

JONATHAN BALCOMBE

From the time I read *In the Shadow of Man* and *Innocent Killers* in high school, Jane has been a source of inspiration and a positive influence on my path as an ethologist and animal advocate. Those books, and the televised documentaries that accompanied them, provided something that the rest of the academic study of animals has largely failed to do: portray wild animals as individuals with biographies, rather than as uncivilized brutes governed by the whims of their evolutionary past.

That, to me, is one of the most important contributions to the evolving human-animal relationship ever made. Credit often goes to Peter Singer for spawning the modern animal rights movement, but a lot of the credit also lies with Jane Goodall. Her ability to popularize the personal lives of animals and her inimitably calm voice and captivating words on their behalf have engaged large swaths of the public, who tend to find philosophers like Singer less accessible.

Jane's pioneering work helped set the stage for and is helping drive the epochal changes we are now seeing in the global struggle for justice for all sentient creatures. Significant moral progress has been made toward liberating Goodall's flagship species: chimpanzee vivisection around the world has nearly been eradicated, most of the chimpanzees held for research by the National Institutes of Health have been retired, and now a lawsuit to have chimps recognized as persons has been filed. More broadly, no longer is it acceptable to dismiss animals as things put here for human ends. No longer are children powerless to effect real change for animals and the environment. And in a growing sector of the planet, no longer is eating animals an apolitical act.

JONATHAN BALCOMBE is an ethologist and author who currently serves as department chair for animal studies with Humane Society University. He lectures on animal behavior and the human-animal relationship.

Jane and Significant Others

PHILIPPA BRAKES

As a child, I visited a wildlife park in Thailand where I saw elephants tied to the spot with heavy ankle chains, a tiger in a cage so small he was unable to turn around or stand up properly, and a single captive pelican who was so miserable in his own cramped surroundings that he had almost plucked himself bare. I complained bitterly to my parents about it for weeks. Eventually, my father told me that if I felt so strongly about this cruelty then I should write to the king of Thailand. I did. Very little came of this first campaign, but the memory of that zoo visit has stayed with me. The experience shaped the nature of the campaigner I was to become: one fueled with righteous indignation.

Years later I began to understand that the very nature of the animals I was trying to protect was far richer and deeper than I could ever have imagined back in Thailand. Reading about Jane Goodall's research made me understand not only the individual and unique personalities of the chimpanzees she'd studied, but also how she had shattered the artificial boundaries between humans and other species. This she managed, while quietly, gently, patiently challenging the dominant academic patriarchy, with its Cartesian desire for researchers to treat other species as unnamed objects rather than sentient individuals.

Today, my work primarily focuses on expanding the conservation agenda beyond species and geographic populations toward protecting individuals with their own unique characteristics, knowledge, and personalities, factors which may also influence the survival of the wider group. Human societies are not composed of identical automatons who merely eat and reproduce. The thoughtful, quietly revolutionary work of Jane and other open-minded primatologists has given us the knowledge and space to look at groups of other highly social mammals, such as elephants, whales, and dolphins, and begin to understand them as multifaceted beings, as individual as each one of us.

This view of the world does not pretend that the lives of other intelligent, sapient beings are not also filled with self-inflicted hardship and melodrama. Instead it highlights the glorious and rich inner lives of these other species. Beyond this compelling new vision that Jane's work was fundamental in bringing to zoology, her gentle but determined approach to conservation and animal welfare has enabled me to let go—a little—of my own righteous indignation. By extending compassion to all other living beings, including those who inflict harm, Jane's approach provides a means and understanding that can bring about a kinder future for all.

Marine biologist PHILIPPA BRAKES is the author of numerous reports, papers, and conference presentations on marine mammal welfare.

Since I Was Eleven Years Old

NATALIE HOUGHTON

I grew up in rural New South Wales and Victoria but spent most of my adult life on remote sheep and cattle stations out of Longreach, in outback Australia. I was eleven years old when I first discovered cruelty to animals. On a hot summer's day, I watched hundreds of sheep suffering and dying in crammed railway carriages. I couldn't understand why the treatment we find abhorrent to people is acceptable for other animals when our capacity to suffer is equal.

Over the years I co-owned and lived on sheep and cattle stations. During that time, I witnessed countless incidents of apathy and violence toward animals—a tolerance for which passed from one generation to another. One day, for example, a station overseer hanged his working kelpie (sheepdog) by her collar on a wire fence in the scorching sun to teach her a lesson, while the young jackeroos (apprentice stockmen) watched and learned. An old truck driver once threw a ewe off the top deck of a road train (a huge multitrailered truck), while the young apprentice truck driver watched and learned. I remember a father once losing his temper with a calf he was trying to brand and thus pressed the hot iron on the calf's delicate pink nose, while his children watched and learned.

I vividly recall a pig-hunting family who'd come to our station regularly to kill feral pigs who would eat our lambs. The parents' disdain for animals was passed on to their sons, who, one day, ran down a pair of emus on their way to a bush ball, cut their heads off, and danced with the long necks and heads at the ball for a laugh.

Common sheep husbandry practices such as castration, ear-marking, mulesing (cutting flesh around the bottom to make scar tissue), and tail-removing were carried out without anesthetic and, although they were obviously extremely painful, were unquestioned by each generation.

Since I was eleven years old, I have known that animals desperately need help, but I couldn't see how I could make a difference. I couldn't see hope . . . until I discovered Humane Education and Jane Goodall's Roots & Shoots program while studying animal welfare at university. Finding a program that fosters love and compassion for all life, promotes the interconnection of all life, and empowers young people to lead the way toward a kinder and sustainable world was what I had been searching for. It has given me hope, purpose, and direction. I immediately joined the Jane Goodall Institute and have been involved in it ever since. I love promoting Jane's program and feel blessed to be able to be a part of this growing movement of people who want a humane, peaceful, and sustainable world.

NATALIE HOUGHTON is chief executive officer of JGI Australia.

JANE AS INSPIRATION

I expect all the contributors to this book will agree that Jane Goodall is an inspiring presence, and many of them have said so. I have selected the essays for this section, though, based on a stronger sense of the concept: not modifying adjective so much as defining noun. Not that she can be *inspiring* so much as that she embraces, in some way, the virtue by being an *inspiration*. That's a rarer thing, and those who feel that way about her would agree with conservation activist Camilla H. Fox, who writes in the opening essay of this section that "few people on this earth continue to inspire and provide hope like Jane Goodall. She is one of those rare souls." Recognized in that way, as a "rare soul," she was (as Hereditary Chief Phil Lane Jr. of the Ihanktonwan Dakota and Chickasaw Nations writes) adopted into the White Swan People and given the sacred name Makoc'e Nakicinzin Winyan, or Defends-the-Land Woman.

But part of what gives her such a powerful effect on people, it might be said, is the way she has become, through the magic machinery of modern media (with images as intimate as the richly scented, glossy pages of the *National Geographic* magazine and as overwhelming as a giant screen in a modern movie theater), both more ubiquitous and larger than life. She may seem like a film star, a modern celebrity.

Celebrity and inspiration have this in common: they gain their power significantly through images. Celebrities are people we know from afar who are brought up close. They thus seem special, and yet simultaneously they can become familiar enough to feel like old friends. Were those same celebrities to be actual old friends, however, we might be disappointed. *People* maga-

zine makes this clear enough. The pretty face and handsome talent for playing a role on screen do not always survive a transition to the role of real life.
Nevertheless, it can be said that much of Jane's power and reputation as an
inspirational figure is reinforced through the circulation of images we all know
so well. We recall the cliché that a picture is worth a thousand words, and we
enter a cathedral to feel inspired by the soaring architecture, the glimmering
glass, and in some traditions the evocative statuary and iconography. Jane is
an icon herself. She "embodies," as actress and singer-songwriter Karen Mok
puts it, the "spirit" of looking "deep into nature" as a way of being. And, yes,
images can inspire us to poetry, but we also want to move beyond glittering
generalities and focus on specifics: mundane details that point to a reality
behind the shimmering surface.

Details are important, and in the case of someone who may *be* an inspiration, who may embody the virtue, we want to know who, when, where, and
what. We want to verify that person's potential to effect creative, transformative changes in others. We want to see the substance, which is the significance of Chief Leonard George's particularized comments—and those of
several other contributors who follow.

Roots & Shoots volunteer Darlene Zavalney declares that "dreams and
wishes that seemed impossible have proven to be quite possible with Jane"—
and supports her contention with examples. Activist, conservationist, and
chocolatier Jon Stocking writes that much of what defines him today was
"personally inspired" by Jane—and gives an instance of how she does it. Dario
Merlo, director of the Jane Goodall Institute in the Democratic Republic of the
Congo, tells of the time Jane "inspired thousands of kids" while bullets and
bombs were exploding six kilometers away. Conservationist and filmmaker Jeff
Orlowski insists that "just knowing that Jane was out there in the world made
it easier for me to keep going. It fueled me, and sustained my energy to make

a difference." Ben Garrod, after describing in substantial detail his own experience of getting to know the person he had as a child "fallen in love with" and been inspired by, tells how the real Jane helped him become a conservationist. To Addison M. Fischer, a supporter of Jane and a board member of the Institute, she is a hero and inspiration because she has proven how much one person with vision and dedication can accomplish. To singer and songwriter Nick Forster, Jane is "a bright beacon of light." He writes, "Jane Goodall travels more and works harder than any musician I know." And for the Founding Director of JGI Australia, Alicia Kennedy, Jane resides as a voice in her head: a voice that says particular, "gently spoken, wise words," creating a daily impact.

But perhaps the best evidence that Jane works her transformative effects on people through something more substantial than a million floating pictures embedded in our collective memory comes from the testimony of magician Gary Haun, who, because he lost his eyesight as a Marine serving in Vietnam many years ago, knows her strictly from a nonvisual perspective. "Jane has a gentle and peaceful soul," Haun declares, although she can also "be as determined as a U.S. Marine when it comes to her concern on issues important to her."

—D. P.

Finding Hope and the Peace of Wild Things

CAMILLA H. FOX

I remember talking to Jane about Wendell Berry's poem "The Peace of Wild Things" and how and where we find that place of hope and rejuvenation amid the despair of it all. We were in Boston, Massachusetts, and I had recently cofounded Boston University Students for the Ethical

Treatment of Animals. Jane was in town giving a talk to an audience of students, many of whom, like me, were working to make this a better world for animals. I will never forget feeling this surge of energy and inspiration after hearing her speak of her experiences studying chimpanzees in Tanzania's Gombe Stream National Park. She spoke of paving new ground in a male-dominated field, of naming animals instead of assigning them numbers, and of trying to talk about animal emotions in a field where such talk was considered blasphemy. She also spoke of finding hope in the face of despair and of never giving up the fight for animals even when the odds were stacked against them.

That happened over twenty years ago. Since then I have worked in the nonprofit sector of animal and environmental protection and have had numerous opportunities to see and hear Jane speak. Few people on this earth continue to inspire and provide hope like Jane Goodall. She is one of those rare souls—on a par with Nelson Mandela and Wangari Maathai. She continues to fly all over the world (300 days a year!) bringing her message to audiences as enthralled as I was twenty years ago with her commitment and compassion for people and animals.

Passion. Commitment. Tenacity. Clarity. Compassion. Empathy. Hope. Inspiration. These are the words that come to mind when I think of Jane Goodall. What a beacon, what an inspiration, what an example of a life well lived.

Thank you, Jane, for all that you do for all beings—four-legged, two-legged, winged, and finned. The world is a better place because of you.

CAMILLA H. FOX is the executive director of Project Coyote, a national nonprofit promoting compassionate conservation and coexistence between people and wildlife.

Defends-the-Land Woman

PHIL LANE JR.

Our beloved elder sister, Dr. Jane Goodall, was ceremonially adopted into the Hinhan Wicasa Tiospaye of the Magaska Ptesan Wicoti, White Swan People of the Ihanktonwan Dakota, one of the Seven Council Fires of the Great Sioux Nation.

Jane's sacred name was given to her by the highly respected and honored Ihanktonwan Dakota hereditary leader and elder, Mato Gi ("Brown Bear") Phil Lane Sr., at the Daybreak Star Indian Cultural Center in Seattle, Washington, on April 3, 2004.

The Sacred Dakota name given to Elder Sister Jane was Makoc'e Nakicinzin Winyan, which translates into English as "Defends-the-Land Woman." This sacred name was given to Elder Sister Jane for her lifetime of dedicated service to our beloved Mother Earth and her loving, compassionate ways of spreading awareness that all life is sacred.

PHIL LANE JR. is hereditary chief of the Ihanktonwan Dakota and Chickasaw Nations. His current focus is supporting the manifestation of the Reunion of the Condor and the Eagle via the Fourth Way across the Americas.

Look Deep into Nature

KAREN MOK

"Look deep into nature, and then you will understand everything better," said Albert Einstein. I cannot think of anyone who embodies this spirit better than Jane Goodall.

Thank you, Jane, for being an inspiration and living proof that we can all live in harmony and be at one with nature.

KAREN MOK (MOK MAN-WAI) is a Hong Kong actress, singer-songwriter, and three-time Golden Melody Award winner.

Providing Hope

LEONARD GEORGE

Jane is the only living being I can think of who, through her work, views, and the Roots & Shoots program, provides hope to people of all ages. Her ideas give us simple tools to do something that will create significant change.

She not only creates awareness on global issues that harm the earth and living creatures but also gives an alternate, healthy way of looking at the issues—and doesn't leave you with the feeling of doom and gloom but a feeling of hope.

Jane Goodall is a true global leader. The world needs more leaders like her, people who have ideas for healthy change that sustains life.

As a woman, she inspires other women by the respect she gets. We so need that because the truth is our women are not respected in the way they need to be. Men are afraid of accepting them as equals, and yet we would be so much better off if we empowered women, and so would the world. Jane is living proof of that.

So thank you, Jane, for giving us a vision of a better world.

LEONARD GEORGE is the primary leader and elected chief of the Tsleil-Waututh Nation in Burrard Inlet, British Columbia. A Coast Salish Aboriginal American, George is a lecturer, humorist, film and script consultant, and actor.

Dreams and Wishes That Seemed Impossible

DARLENE ZAVALNEY

Jane has changed my life in so many ways, I doubt I realize them all. Dreams and wishes that seemed impossible have proven to be quite possible with Jane. Her passion for our planet and her message of personal empowerment have given me confidence I never knew I had.

Jane's support gave me the courage to accomplish things I never dreamed. With the help of a great team of volunteers and little money, I have produced or helped to produce about a dozen Roots & Shoots festivals. Our largest brought 10,000 people to the Santa Monica Pier. Last January our event raised $40,000 for Roots & Shoots. We had never attempted a fundraiser before, but Jane believed in us and gave us the opportunity and the inspiration. We are hoping to do more.

For as long as I can remember, I have had a fire in my belly to do something, to make a difference. When I saw the redwood forest and Yosemite National Park for the first time, I was hooked. I not only wanted to protect all this natural beauty, I felt I had to! The passion I feel for the environment of our own country now spills over to the rest of the planet.

Thanks to Jane, I am making a difference. I have been elected to our local neighborhood council, working to make our communities cleaner, greener, and safer. I would not have had the courage to do this before meeting Jane.

I love Jane so very much. To me, she is Mother Earth. More than that, she is a very dear friend.

DARLENE ZAVALNEY is the owner of a promotional marketing company. She has worked since 1996 to promote and develop Roots & Shoots, along with her husband, John.

To My Inspiration

JON STOCKING

Dear Jane,

Much of what defines me today you've personally inspired.

I remember I asked you once, after you'd seen so much bad in the world—from the inhumane way we treat ourselves (after your post-9/11 tour), to the inhumane way we treat our relatives (e.g., the Air Force chimpanzees)—how you always manage to maintain such a hopeful and positive outlook. You replied ever so simply, "Because I must." It wasn't a defiant declaration, a challenge to the mass majority, or a soapbox chest thump. Rather, it was a peaceful "This is who I am, who I've become, and who I must continue to be." Yours is such a meaningful lead-by-example virtue carried with such pure love, grace, and dignity—something I will always strive to emulate myself.

Aristotle said, "Friendship is a single soul dwelling in two bodies." There are thousands of people today you have touched so intimately who feel your friendship in such a way. No matter how busy your schedule is or what part of the world you are in, you always find time to pick up the phone and call. And after every conversation, after every time we've been together, I'm always a better person and a single soul with you.

Happy Birthday to my inspiration.

JON STOCKING (aka Chocolate Jon) founded the Endangered Species Chocolate Company and the Republic of Pie. He has been a friend of Jane's for twenty-one years.

She Inspired Thousands of Kids

DARIO MERLO

It was July 2013, and the United Nations and Congolese army forces were fighting a rebel army from M23 just outside Goma, in the eastern Democratic Republic of the Congo. The M23 rebels were trying to take the town. People from UN security and the British embassy had previously advised that we not let Jane visit, but who's going to tell Jane what to do? She insisted, saying that if our staff was still operating, there was no reason why she couldn't come.

When she arrived, I gave her a security update. She was, of course, in the most secure hotel. The UN and embassy staff were informed of her presence. She had access to the lake, and a boat was ready to pick her up any time the situation escalated. Still, wars can be unpredictable. She had planned, for the next day, to speak at the biggest university of Goma and in front of several Roots & Shoots groups, but the war was now at our door. So I asked Jane if she wanted to do that, and she said: "Of course I will do the speech." I said that it might be more secure to go south to the town of Bukavu, but she said, "If this is the situation you are living in, I would rather stay so I can understand what your daily life is like." That's when I understood how much Jane cares about every individual, how tough she is, and how committed she is to her mission.

She gave a brilliant speech and inspired thousands of kids with a positive message while, at that very time, we could hear the noise of bombs and bullets exploding only six kilometers away. A few days later, Goma was taken by the rebels, but Jane's speech that day inspired us and gave us a wonderful example of courage and compassion.

DARIO MERLO is director of the Jane Goodall Institute in the Democratic Republic of the Congo.

Chasing Jane and *Chasing Ice*

JEFF ORLOWSKI

Jane Goodall and I met three days after September 11, 2001. I was a senior in high school, and our building was located just four blocks away from the World Trade Center towers in Manhattan. As editor in chief of the school paper, I asked Jane if she would write something for our student body, who had just experienced this terrible tragedy. She wrote a piece called "Why We Should Still Have Hope."

Over the years, I kept seeing Jane and kept hearing her stories of hope. Whether it was while I was home, at college, or living abroad, I always tried to work my schedule around her travel plans. I have seen her give close to a hundred talks, sometimes doing half a dozen lectures in a day. And no matter how many times I have heard the same stories, they never got old. Her message—that one person *can* make a difference—kept getting drilled into my brain. I internalized the mantra: each one of us has a part to play, and we all need to work together to make a difference.

After college, I started working on a project that would eventually lead to my first feature film, *Chasing Ice*. The process of making this documentary about climate change and featuring time-lapse film of glacial retreat around the world was one of the most brutal and artistically trying experiences in my life—and, of course, the film was rejected from countless film festivals during the early stages of editing. But Jane's story was constantly in the back of my mind: if I don't do something about this, if I don't tell this story, then nobody else will. A sense of responsibility surrounded those years, and ultimately my team and I kept striving to make the film as good as possible.

Ultimately *Chasing Ice* premiered at Sundance, went on to hundreds of film festivals, and was nominated for an Academy Award. I spent over a year and a half touring with the film, trying to inform the public about the reality of climate change. I was traveling from city to city, hotel to hotel, repeating the same message and answering the same questions. I burned out several times over, and the stress had a huge impact on my personal life. But in the back of my mind, I kept seeing this nearly eighty-year-old woman who seemed to survive on just toast and coffee while being on the road for over 300 days a year. I felt that I had no right to complain—that my exhaustion was nothing compared to what Jane has endured for decades. If she could sacrifice her own comfort for the sake of making an impact, then I should be able to as well. In a weird way, just knowing that Jane was out there in the world made it easier for me to keep going. It fueled me and sustained my energy to make a difference.

JEFF ORLOWSKI, director and producer of the Academy Award–nominated film *Chasing Ice*, is working to leverage the film and the evidence of climate change to spark social and political action in the United States and around the world.

Chimps, I Think

BEN GARROD

"It's the lady who works with animals. . . . chimps, I think." So started a night that would ultimately change my life. I was a third-year undergraduate, studying animal behavior.

To earn extra cash, I worked at the university faculty club as a silver service waiter, and luckily, I was often on the "top table." After asking what tonight's event was and getting this response, I'm happy to admit that my mind went into meltdown. I knew it could only be one person: Jane Goodall.

Jane was a huge inspiration to me growing up. I had countless magazines with her splashed over the covers—representing a lens into the beautiful world of our nearest primate relatives. I had been to Africa three years earlier, had seen wild chimpanzees, and had fallen in love with them. Now, I was about to actually serve Jane. After a quick but essential pep talk to my mum on the phone, I was ready. It was a charity evening to raise funds for chimpanzee conservation, and the guests filed in.

She came in toward the end and that was it. The panic set in. What if I spill soup on Jane Goodall? As I started to serve her, she turned around and gave me that smile of hers that I now know so well.

"Hello, what's your name?" she asked.

After I stammered my name, she replied, "Mine's Jane"—to which I could only say, "I know."

After regaining control of my key motor skills, I continued serving her—as, unbelievably, we started chatting. I finally built up the courage to ask for advice on how I could work in Africa with chimps, and she did something I shall never forget. She touched my hand and looked at me. In fact, she seemed to look right into me. It must have only been for a few seconds, but it seemed like an eternity. She broke away and said she'd see what she could do.

A few months later, I was living in Uganda, running a large chimpanzee conservation project for her. I've since worked all around the world with primates, am on various primate society councils, and am a trustee for JGI UK. This is all thanks to Jane. She not only inspired me; she believed in me. She gave me an opportunity that I never imagined was possible, and I have strived to do her proud through my work. Numerous times now, we've been at events together, and Jane has introduced me by saying, "He started off as my waiter, you know." Not only has Jane shaped my life immeasurably, but I have seen her touch the lives of countless individuals she's met.

On behalf of all of those people, Jane, I want to thank you for believing in us as we believe in you.

BEN GARROD studies primate evolution and is involved in primate conservation, acting as a council member for Primate Society (UK) and as a trustee for JGI UK.

You Are My Hero

ADDISON M. FISCHER

Dear Jane,

You are my friend and inspiration. Sometimes, when I become distressed over the state of the world and the things our civilization is doing to us and our planet, I think of your optimism, your undaunted attitude, and your words: "We cannot give up; we must succeed; we will succeed." And they renew my spirit.

It's a reflection of your dedication and stamina that you can travel 300 days a year and yet create so many books and films. You have proven how much one person with vision and dedication can accomplish. You are my hero.

ADDISON M. FISCHER founded Fischer International Systems Corporation. Since 2005 he has worked closely with Jane Goodall, and he now serves as a board member of the Jane Goodall Institute.

A Bright Beacon of Light

NICK FORSTER

Jane Goodall is a bright beacon of light radiating around the world. With her passion for animals and her spirit of adventure, she chose a path that helped create an almost mythical persona: a beautiful, smart woman living in the wilds with chimpanzees. You can't make that stuff up (even though they tried to with Tarzan and Jane).

Of course, she became one of the world's most experienced and respected scientists in primate research. But far more importantly, Jane helped us all see animals as fellow travelers, not deaf-mute resources to be exploited. She showed us the value of habitat and its delicate interrelatedness to all things.

Most of all, I love the fact that she is universally appealing. For every age, class, and culture, in every language, and in every country, she can connect with a crowd and leave them inspired. She makes all of us recalibrate our priorities and remember that we are here only briefly and that our impact on the planet can and should be lighter.

Jane Goodall travels more and works harder than any musician I know. Like most musicians, she has a lot of fun along the way. I'm so glad that our paths have crossed so often, and I'm honored to have gotten to know her.

NICK FORSTER, founding member of the bluegrass band Hot Rize and founder/host of *eTown*, is a multi-instrumentalist, singer, and songwriter.

The Voice in My Head

ALICIA KENNEDY

As a child growing up in the '60s and '70s, I followed Jane Goodall's journey through the stories I read in *National Geographic*. Africa was a long way away from my hometown, Adelaide, South Australia—but Jane became one of my key inspirations to pursue a career serving animals. I lost track of her for a while, but her story returned to my life in 2002 when a friend loaned me Jane's book *Reason for Hope*. At that time I was a busy mum with three young daughters, all of us living as expats in China and feeling overwhelmed by the problems our planet faces. *Why should I bother doing anything if nobody else cares?* That was how I felt until I read *Reason for Hope*.

Since then, Jane has become the voice in my head (at least *one* of them). Or is it my voice that aligns so closely with hers? Who knows? What I do know is that Jane Goodall has become a guiding force in my life. I rarely see or speak with Jane, but her gently spoken, wise words influence me daily.

"Do what you can when you can with the time and resources you have. That will make a difference. That will be enough." Jane shared those words with me at the end of our first meeting, in Beijing, 2004. As an Australian living in China and passionate about Roots & Shoots, I started the program in our international school but noticed that there was not a global office in Australia. Why not? I wondered. So when Jane visited China, I campaigned hard to meet with her. I asked, "What about Australia?" She explained that nobody had started it there yet, to which I replied, "I'll help." This conversation marked a turning point in my life. Seeing JGI established in Australia has occupied many of my hours and much of my energy over the past ten years. It has been an incredible journey filled with beautiful connections, moments of joy, and many challenges.

"We must never, ever give up," I hear her say. So on we go, forging ahead in the face of adversity, after hearing story after story of disaster and suffering for animals and people. At times we face burnout, utterly overwhelmed by it all—and then we find the resilience and hope that Jane talks about. The four reasons for hope: human ingenuity, the indomitable human spirit, the resilience of nature, and the energy and creativity of youth. I have experienced the energy and creativity of youth many times—young people who are driven to create a better world, their hearts connected to their minds. That is where my hope lies, through the many young people I continue to connect with through JGI.

"Discover your gifts and passions, and use these to follow your dreams while creating a better world for animals, people, and the environment." Those are Jane's words, and I continue to share them far and wide. With my daughters it has become my mantra. Jane Goodall has not only been an influential force in my life, but I am seeing my daughters all blossom into their own talents while creating a better world.

ALICIA KENNEDY, veterinarian, is the founding director of the JGI Australia. She is also the mother of three daughters who have grown up with Roots & Shoots.

Dr. J and Mr. H

GARY HAUN

Dr. Jane and I went on a walk through the Sonora Desert in Tucson, Arizona. She told me to listen to the sounds of the desert so I could tell the Roots & Shoots kids about my experience. Then she picked up a piece of dried-out cactus and gave it to me to feel. I carry it with me today and consider it one of the most precious things I have. You see, Jane taught me that it's not about how much money we have in our pockets. It's about how much love and concern we have for one another and how it's up to us to make this home we call planet Earth a better place.

Among other things dear to me are the notes that Jane would send from her beloved Gombe. She would describe in detail the activities of the various chimps. You could tell she loved them very much. She would describe the surroundings, such as Lake Tanganyika during sunset, almost like a poet. As she put it, "It looks like diamonds dancing on the water." Jane has a gentle and peaceful soul. However, make no doubt about it, Dr. Jane can be as determined as a U.S. Marine when it comes to issues important to her. The lesson here is that we all should be concerned with issues of our environment and the beings who live in it. The world would be such a peaceful place in which to live if we followed the path of Dr. Jane.

When I first met Jane at a Roots & Shoots Summit in Tulsa, Oklahoma, it seemed as though we had known each other for all our lives. I think she has this charming effect on everyone she meets. She has a way of making people think, What can I do to make the world a better place?

It is hard to think of Jane without thinking about her mom, Vanne. What a sweet, kind, and lovely woman. I talked with her on the phone sometimes when I called Jane at home during Christmas. Vanne always seemed happy and could make people happy just by talking to her. What a remarkable person—just like her daughter! Jane did not have to look far for a role model on how to live life.

Maybe because I'm blind, Jane once asked me to write to a blind kid who was terminally ill. The kid's mom told me that Jane had inspired him so much. It was the first time the mom ever saw her son smile, and therein is the real magic of Dr. Jane Goodall. She has taught me and thousands of others that it is not what we see with our eyes. It's what we see with our hearts.

Jane has been such an inspiration for me that one time I decided to give her a little gift, and so I ordered a stuffed toy chimpanzee from a catalog. This, I thought, could be a small companion during the lonely and often difficult times when she travels. But when I handed the chimp to Jane, she said he looked nothing like a chimp. I asked her, "How would you know?" She said the toy animal had a tail, and chimps don't have tails. I said Mr. H—which is what we named him—had to look like a chimp because the toy catalog said he did! She laughed when I told her that, and I like to hear Jane laugh. When she does, it somehow lets me know the world is OK or, at least, doing better. I told her that Mr. H is magical, but I know the real magic is in Dr. Jane. She gives people the most valuable thing on the planet—*hope.*

GARY HAUN, a former Marine, performs magic around the world as the Amazing Haundini. He is the father of Mr. H.

About the Editors

DALE PETERSON writes full time and teaches on occasion in the English Department at Tufts University. His twenty books include Jane Goodall's only full biography, *Jane Goodall: The Woman Who Redefined Man*; two edited volumes of Goodall's letters, *Africa in My Blood* and *Beyond Innocence*; and the coauthored *Visions of Caliban: On Chimpanzees and People*. www.dalepetersonauthor.com.

MARC BEKOFF is a former professor of ecology and evolutionary biology at the University of Colorado, Boulder, an ambassador for Jane Goodall's Roots & Shoots program, and a member of the Ethics Committee of the Jane Goodall Institute. He and Goodall cofounded the organization Ethologists for the Ethical Treatment of Animals: Citizens for Responsible Animal Behavior Studies in 2000. He is the author of, most recently, *Rewilding Our Hearts: Building Pathways of Compassion and Coexistence*, *Why Dogs Hump and Bees Get Depressed: The Fascinating Science of Animal Intelligence, Emotions, Friendship, and Conservation*, as well as *The Emotional Lives of Animals*, the award-winning children's book *Jasper's Story: Saving Moon Bears* (with Jill Robinson), and *The Ten Trusts: What We Must Do to Care for the Animals We Love*, which he coauthored with Goodall. He lives in Boulder, Colorado. www.marcbekoff .com and www.ethologicalethics.org.